# Oxford SKILLS WORLD
# Reading
## with Writing
# 5

## Elise Pritchard

OXFORD
UNIVERSITY PRESS

**OXFORD**
UNIVERSITY PRESS

198 Madison Avenue
New York, NY 10016 USA

Great Clarendon Street, Oxford, OX2 6DP, United Kingdom

Oxford University Press is a department of the University of Oxford.
It furthers the University's objective of excellence in research, scholarship,
and education by publishing worldwide. Oxford is a registered trade
mark of Oxford University Press in the UK and in certain other countries

ISBN: 978 0 19 411354 0 Student Book with Workbook

Printed in China

This book is printed on paper from certified and well-managed sources

ACKNOWLEDGMENTS

*Oxford University Press would like to thank all of the teachers whose opinions helped to
inform this series, and in particular, the following reviewers*: Soo Ah Chung, Hwarang
Elementary School; Marta Juanet, Betania-patmos; Sedef Toksöz Kaykın,
Denizli Pamukkale Unv Egitim Vakfi okullari (PEV Koleji); Jeehee Moon,
T.T.R.; Jacob Rod, WILS Language School; Yuechun Wang, Phonenix City
International School

*Cover illustration and main character illustrations by*: Shane McGowan/The
Organisation

*Back cover photograph*: Oxford University Press building/David Fisher

**Student Book**

*Illustrations by*: Scott Angle/Carole Newman & Associates pp.34, 37–39, 43, 58;
Mattia Cerato/MB Artists pp.20, 27–28; Peter Francis/MB Artists pp.76, 81,
83–85; Chris Jones/Byer-Sprinzeles Agency pp.44, 72; John Kurtz pp.103, 107,
113; Anthony Lewis/MB Artists pp.11, 13–14, 17, 45, 67, 71; Juan Moreno/MB
Artists pp.62, 65–66, 73; Jomike Tejido/MB Artists pp.48, 55–57, 86–88

*The Publishers would like to thank the following for their kind permission to reproduce
photographs and other copyright material*: 123rf: Cover (Paraglider/Thomas
Zagler), pp.29 (rabbit hopping/Geza Farkas), 30 (animals at water hole/Zdenek
Maly), 41 (room in ice hotel/Israel Horga Garcia), 51 (Hawaiian canyon/
Sheri Armstrong), 60 (sandcastle/pogonici), 62–63 (catfish/elf0724), 69 (tuba/
alephcomo); Alamy: pp.20–21 (African animals/Panther Media GmbH),
70 (woman playing trombone/Blend Images); Getty: pp.16 (girl on laptop/JGI/
Tom Grill), 20 (jaguar/Javier Fernández Sánchez), 23 (jaguar/Javier Fernández
Sánchez), 34–35 (robot vacuuming/Maciej Frolow); Oxford University Press:
pp.9 (food groups wheel/ifong), 62 (trumpet/Furtseff), 69 (trombone/seen0001),
(trumpet/Furtseff); Shutterstock: 6–7 (fruit stall/NFKenyon), 10 (woman
eating chocolates/Yuri Shevtsov), 15 (curry dishes/stocksolutions), 18 (coffee
beans/deanmoriarty44), 24 (polar bear/Alexey Seafarer), 25 (lizard/Roman
Tarasevych), 31 (butterflies/Anake Seenadee), 32 (dolphin/Halyna Parinova),
40 (Ice background/Valentyn Volkov), 42 (men transporting ice/junrong),
46 (boy walking dog/Ljupco Smokovski), 48–49 (Atacama desert/Ksenia
Ragozina), 52 (woodland trail/Roman Khomlyak), 53 (elephants drinking/
Fabian Plock), 54 (Old map/Andrey_Kuzmin), 59 (Japanese gardens/Sean
Pavone), 74 (Footprints on beach/Pawel Kazmierczak), 76–77 (Egyptian fresco/
Jakub Kyncl), 79 (men on camels/Don Mammoser), 80 (citadel/Repina Valeriya)

**Workbook**

*Illustrations by*: Scott Angle/Carole Newman & Associates p.99; Lalena Fisher
p.105; John Kurtz pp.107, 113; Anthony Lewis/MB Artists p.93

*The Publishers would like to thank the following for their kind permission to reproduce
photographs and other copyright material*: 123rf: p.97 (springbok/Zdenek Maly);
Getty: p.101 (robot vacuuming/Maciej Frolow); Oxford University Press:
p.91 (healthy snacks/ifong); Shutterstock: pp.95 (polar bear/Alexey Seafarer),
109 (puppy listening/Gladskikh) Tatiana), 111 (Chinese street food/Matt Grant)

# Table of Contents

Hi! I'm Olly.

Hi, I'm Molly!

# Introduction

## Welcome to Oxford Skills World

Oxford Skills World: Reading with Writing is a flexible paired skills course that takes students on a journey toward independent learning, providing them with strategies and support to reach their goals.

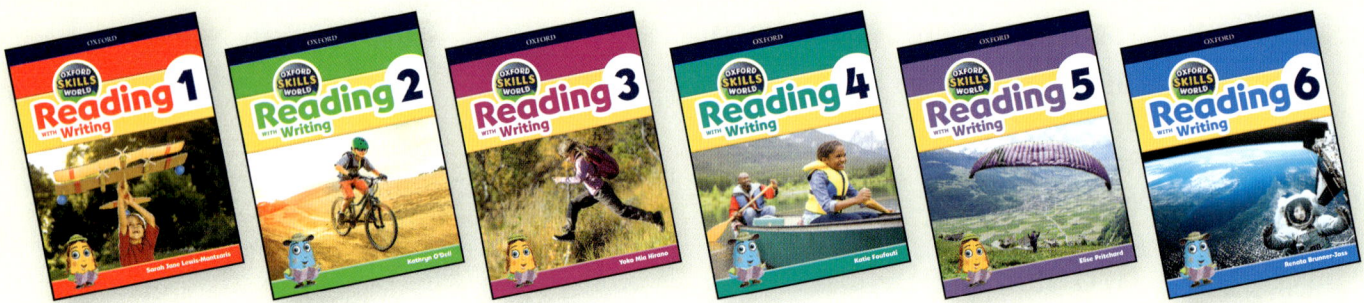

### For Students

- Student Book / Workbook
- Student's website with downloadable audio and extra resources
  www.oup.com/elt/oxfordskillsworld

### For Teachers

- Downloadable Teacher's Pack with instructional support, assessment, professional development videos, projects, and writing resources
- Classroom Presentation Tool
- Teacher's website with downloadable audio and extra resources
  www.oup.com/elt/teacher/oxfordskillsworld

## Be the Leader on Your Skills Adventure!

Hi! We're Olly and Molly, your skills adventure guides. We help you reach your goals by introducing new reading and writing strategies, asking helpful questions, and giving friendly reminders. Most importantly, we cheer you on every step of the way! Let's go!

# Quick Guide

## Inside Each Topic

### Topic Opener

Theme-based topics provide high-interest content relevant to students' lives.

**My Goals** introduces students to the objectives of each unit in the topic.*

Fun characters, Olly and Molly, encourage 21st century skills like critical thinking, collaboration, and communication.

Students answer questions to activate prior knowledge and think critically.

### Get Ready to Read • Read

**Reading Goals** are strategies students can apply to any text.

Olly and Molly support students as they apply **Reading Goals** to each text.

Before they read, students practice applying the unit's **Reading Goal** and identify new vocabulary.

At the end of each lesson, students assess the progress they are making toward achieving their goals.

*Each topic contains two thematically related units.

# Quick Guide

## Understand

Students increase their comprehension of the text by applying reading strategies to what they have read.

Students complete activities focused on reading comprehension and critical thinking.

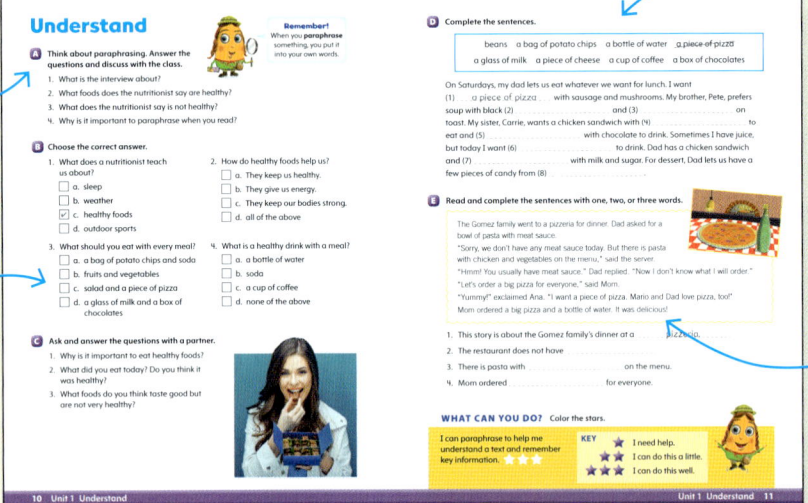

Vocabulary application activities strengthen students' comprehension of the unit's new language.

Additional texts and activities prepare students for task types found on standardized exams, such as Cambridge English Qualifications for young learners.

## Reading Check

With helpful reminders from the Olly and Molly, students apply the **Reading Goals** from both units to a new text.

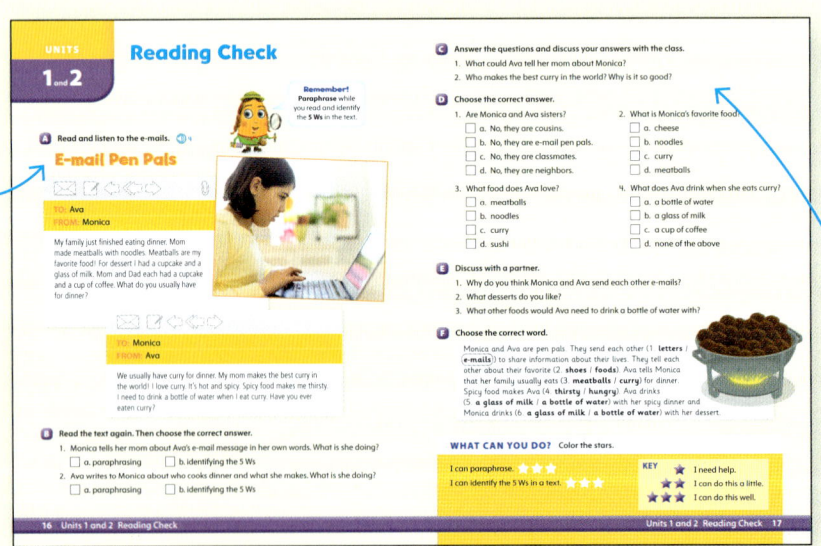

Students complete activities to boost comprehension and vocabulary application.

# Get Ready to Write • Write

**Writing Goals** prepare students to write in different genres.

**Writing Tips** provide guidance on grammar, punctuation, and mechanics and help students write fluently and accurately.

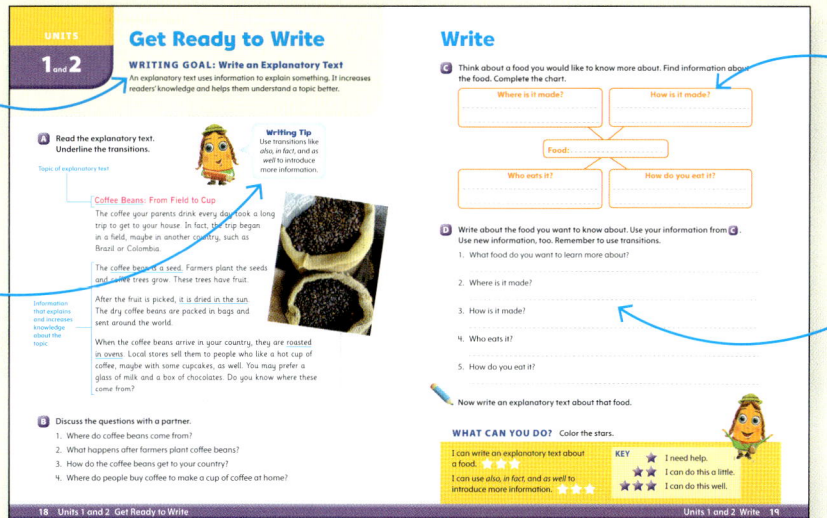

Students use graphic organizers to organize their thoughts for their own writing.

Thought-provoking questions help students generate ideas they will use in their own writing.

# Workbook

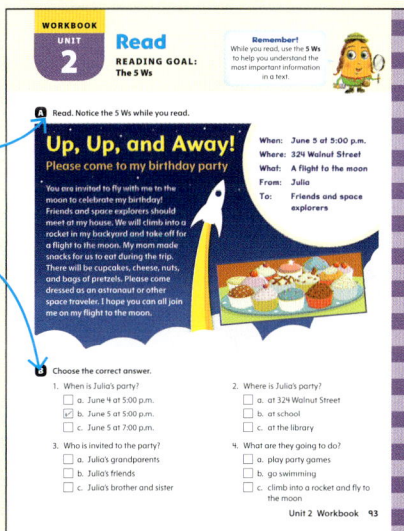

Workbook pages at the end of the book provide more opportunities for students to apply their **Reading Goals** and boost comprehension.

Additional activities provide extra opportunities for vocabulary comprehension and usage.

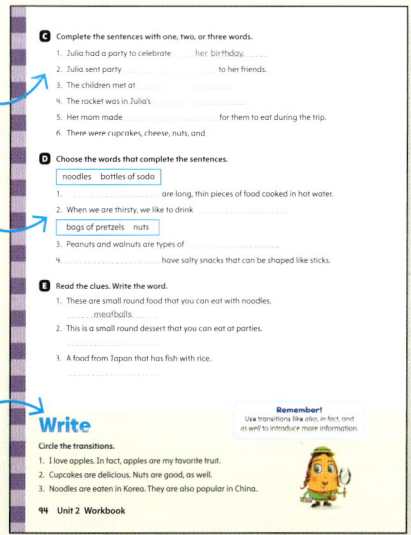

Students apply the topic's **Writing Tip** to ensure proper usage in their own writing.

# Let's Eat!

## MY GOALS

### UNIT 1

- Read the interview *Healthy Foods, Healthy Bodies*

- Paraphrase

### UNIT 2

- Read the story *Our Class Party*

- Use the 5 Ws

### WRITE

- Write an explanatory text

 **A** Look at the picture.

1. What is for sale in the market?

2. Which of these fruits have you tried?

## Unusual Fruits

This is a fresh fruit market in Thailand. Many unusual fruit like rambutans, star fruit, and dragon fruit grow in Thailand. The rambutan is oval with soft red hairs. The star fruit is green and looks like a star when you cut it. The pink dragon fruit with black spots is called that because old stories say they came from fire-breathing dragons!

**B** Read the text.

1. Where is this market?
2. What unusual fruits does it sell?
3. What do old stories say about the dragon fruit?

**Think, Pair, Share**
What fruits do you like to eat? Why?

# Read

## READING GOAL: Paraphrase

Paraphrasing is putting something into your own words. You can paraphrase something you read or something someone says. When you read, paraphrase to help you understand a text and remember key information.

## Get Ready

**A** Read the paragraph below. Choose the correct paraphrase.

Bobby uses apples, bananas, and grapes to make smoothies. He peels the fruit and drops it in the blender. *Swoosh!* In seconds he has a delicious smoothie!

☐ a. Bobby makes smoothies with apples, bananas, and grapes.

☐ b. Smoothies can be made with different fruits.

**B** Find the key words in the interview. Look up the words you don't know in your dictionary.

**C** Read and listen to the interview *Healthy Foods, Healthy Bodies.* 🔊 2

# Healthy Foods, Healthy Bodies

| | | |
|---|---|---|
| | **Student:** | I am happy to introduce Ms. Potter. She is a nutritionist in our community. Nutritionists teach us about healthy foods. |
| 5 | **Ms. Potter:** | Hello, students. To stay healthy, you need to eat healthy foods. Healthy foods give us energy and keep our bodies strong. |
| 10 | **Student:** | Ms. Potter, can you please tell us about some healthy foods we should eat? |
| 15 | **Ms. Potter:** | Of course! First, you should eat fruits and vegetables with every meal. Rice and beans are healthy, too. |
| | **Student:** | What about a bag of potato chips? |
| | **Ms. Potter:** | Potatoes are vegetables, but potato chips are not a healthy food. |
| | **Student:** | What about pizza? |
| 20 | **Ms. Potter:** | Once in a while, a piece of pizza with a salad is OK. It sure is delicious, but it's not very healthy. |
| 25 | **Student:** | I drink a glass of milk with meals and snacks, but my mom likes to have a cup of coffee. Is that okay? |

**Ms. Potter:** It's better to drink a glass of milk or a bottle of water with meals and snacks.

**Student:** You said snacks. I like to eat a box of chocolates for a snack. Is that healthy?

30 **Ms. Potter:** Chocolate is delicious but not healthy for your body. You should try a piece of cheese instead. That will give you energy and keep you strong!

What is this interview about? Tell about it in your own words.

---

**WHAT CAN YOU DO?**   Color the stars.

I can read the interview and paraphrase it.
⭐⭐⭐

I can understand all the key words.
⭐⭐⭐

**KEY**
⭐ I need help.
⭐⭐ I can do this a little.
⭐⭐⭐ I can do this well.

# Understand

**Remember!**
When you **paraphrase** something, you put it into your own words.

**A** Think about paraphrasing. Answer the questions and discuss with the class.

1. What is the interview about?
2. What foods does the nutritionist say are healthy?
3. What does the nutritionist say is not healthy?
4. Why is it important to paraphrase when you read?

**B** Choose the correct answer.

1. What does a nutritionist teach us about?
   - ☐ a. sleep
   - ☐ b. weather
   - ☑ c. healthy foods
   - ☐ d. outdoor sports

2. How do healthy foods help us?
   - ☐ a. They keep us healthy.
   - ☐ b. They give us energy.
   - ☐ c. They keep our bodies strong.
   - ☐ d. all of the above

3. What should you eat with every meal?
   - ☐ a. a bag of potato chips and soda
   - ☐ b. fruits and vegetables
   - ☐ c. salad and a piece of pizza
   - ☐ d. a glass of milk and a box of chocolates

4. What is a healthy drink with a meal?
   - ☐ a. a bottle of water
   - ☐ b. soda
   - ☐ c. a cup of coffee
   - ☐ d. none of the above

**C** Ask and answer the questions with a partner.

1. Why is it important to eat healthy foods?
2. What did you eat today? Do you think it was healthy?
3. What foods do you think taste good but are not very healthy?

## D  Complete the sentences.

> beans    a bag of potato chips    a bottle of water    ~~a piece of pizza~~
>
> a glass of milk    a piece of cheese    a cup of coffee    a box of chocolates

On Saturdays, my dad lets us eat whatever we want for lunch. I want
(1) _____a piece of pizza_____ with sausage and mushrooms. My brother, Pete, prefers
soup with black (2) _____ and (3) _____ on
toast. My sister, Carrie, wants a chicken sandwich with (4) _____ to
eat and (5) _____ with chocolate to drink. Sometimes I have juice,
but today I want (6) _____ to drink. Dad has a chicken sandwich
and (7) _____ with milk and sugar. For dessert, Dad lets us have a
few pieces of candy from (8) _____.

## E  Read and complete the sentences with one, two, or three words.

> The Gomez family went to a pizzeria for dinner. Dad asked for a
> bowl of pasta with meat sauce.
>
> "Sorry, we don't have any meat sauce today. But there is pasta
> with chicken and vegetables on the menu," said the server.
>
> "Hmm! You usually have meat sauce." Dad replied. "Now I don't know what I will order."
>
> "Let's order a big pizza for everyone," said Mom.
>
> "Yummy!" exclaimed Ana. "I want a piece of pizza. Mario and Dad love pizza, too!"
>
> Mom ordered a big pizza and a bottle of water. It was delicious!

1.  This story is about the Gomez family's dinner at a _____ pizzeria. _____

2.  The restaurant does not have _____

3.  There is pasta with _____ on the menu.

4.  Mom ordered _____ for everyone.

## WHAT CAN YOU DO?  Color the stars.

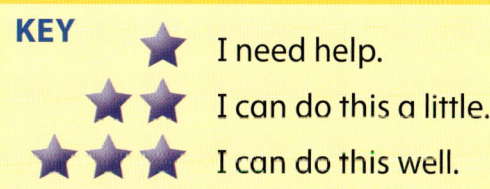

I can paraphrase to help me
understand a text and remember
key information. ⭐⭐⭐

KEY   ⭐ I need help.
      ⭐⭐ I can do this a little.
      ⭐⭐⭐ I can do this well.

## READING GOAL: Use the 5 Ws

The 5 Ws are *who*, *what*, *when*, *where*, and *why*.
When you read, use the 5 Ws to understand the most important information in the story.

## Get Ready

**A**  Read the sentence below. Choose the correct answer.

Kemal rides his bike to school on Wednesdays.

1. Who rides his bike to school?
   ☑ a. Kemal
   ☐ b. to school

2. What does Kemal ride to school?
   ☐ a. Wednesdays
   ☐ b. his bike

3. Where does Kemal ride his bike?
   ☐ a. his bike
   ☐ b. to school

**B**  Find the 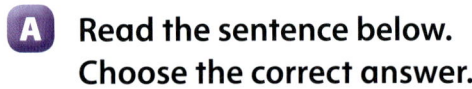 key words in the story. Look up the words you don't know in your dictionary.

**C**  Read and listen to the story *Our Class Party*. 🔊 3

# Our Class Party

The senior class is planning an end-of-year party. It will be in the gym on Friday afternoon. Amy and Samy are organizing the food and drinks. Some classmates have already told
5  them what they are going to bring.

Karen is baking **cupcakes**. She is making one little cake for each person at the party. Bill is bringing **bags of pretzels** and a bowl of nuts. Walnuts and peanuts are some of his
10  favorite **nuts**.

"What about Mia and Jae?" Samy asks.

"Mia is bringing **sushi**. I love those little balls of rice with fish inside," says Amy. "And Jae is preparing **noodles** with tiny **meatballs** on
15  top. He makes them just like they do in Italy! Everyone says they're delicious."

"I'm bringing **curry**," Samy exclaims. "My mom makes the best curry in the world!"

Friday afternoon Amy and Samy are in the gym
20  putting the food on the table. Everything looks
delicious. "We have a lot of food," Amy says. "But are
there enough bottles of soda?"

"No," Samy replies. "I think we need a few more."

"That's okay," replies Amy. "We have water and juice.
25  And now everyone is arriving. Look, they are starting
to sing karaoke. Can you hear the music? It's going to
be a fantastic party!"

What are the
**5 Ws** of the
story (*who,
what, when,
where, why*)?

## WHAT CAN YOU DO?   Color the stars.

I can read the story and find the 5 Ws.

I can understand all the key words.

**KEY**

 I need help.

 I can do this a little.

★★★ I can do this well.

# Understand

**A** Think about the 5 Ws. Answer the questions and discuss with the class.

1. Where and when is the party?

2. Why is the class planning a party?

3. Who is bringing food and what will they bring?

4. Why is it important to use the 5 Ws while you read?

**B** Read. Choose **T** for **True** and **F** for **False**.

1. The class is having a party for the teacher's birthday.    T    (F)

2. The party will be in the gym on a Friday afternoon.    T    F

3. Mia is bringing sushi and Jae will bring meatballs.    T    F

4. Samy is preparing noodles.    T    F

5. Amy's mom makes good curry.    T    F

6. There will be a lot of food at the party.    T    F

7. There are too many bottles of soda.    T    F

8. The students will sing karaoke at the party.    T    F

**C** Ask and answer the questions with a partner.

1. What drinks will they have at the party?

2. Which foods at the party would you like to try? Why?

3. What will the students do at the party?

4. What party could your class plan?

**D** Choose the correct answer.

1. In line 6, *cupcakes* are
   - [ ] a. a kind of cookie.
   - [ ] b. small cakes for one person.
   - [ ] c. large cakes about the size of a pizza.
   - [ ] d. vegetables.

2. In line 9, walnuts and peanuts are types of
   - [ ] a. baking.
   - [ ] b. cupcakes.
   - [ ] c. bags.
   - [ ] d. nuts.

3. In line 12, what is *sushi*?
   - [ ] a. small balls of rice with fish inside
   - [ ] b. a noodle dish from Korea
   - [ ] c. a meat dish from Japan
   - [ ] d. a type of cookie

4. In line 14, *meatballs* are
   - [ ] a. a type of nut.
   - [ ] b. a food people make in Italy.
   - [ ] c. a small cake for one person.
   - [ ] d. small pieces of rice with fish inside.

**E** Read the text. Then read the questions and choose the correct answer.

## What Is Curry?

Many foods, like sushi and noodles, come from Asia. India is known for its curry dishes. Today, people all around the world eat curry dishes.

Curry is a meal for breakfast, lunch, or dinner. Curries can be made with fish, meat, chicken, or vegetables. Many curries are made with chili peppers, so be careful — some are very hot and spicy. They are so popular because they are delicious!

1. Where do curry dishes come from?
   - [ ] a. Korea
   - [ ] b. India
   - [ ] c. Japan

2. What makes some curries very spicy?
   - [ ] a. chicken
   - [ ] b. vegetables
   - [ ] c. chili peppers

**WHAT CAN YOU DO?** Color the stars.

I can use the 5 Ws to help me understand the most important information in a text. ⭐⭐⭐

KEY
⭐ I need help.
⭐⭐ I can do this a little.
⭐⭐⭐ I can do this well.

# Reading Check

**Remember!**
**Paraphrase** while you read and identify the **5 Ws** in the text.

**A** Read and listen to the e-mails.  4

## E-mail Pen Pals

**TO:** Ava
**FROM:** Monica

My family just finished eating dinner. Mom made meatballs with noodles. Meatballs are my favorite food! For dessert I had a cupcake and a glass of milk. Mom and Dad each had a cupcake and a cup of coffee. What do you usually have for dinner?

**TO:** Monica
**FROM:** Ava

We usually have curry for dinner. My mom makes the best curry in the world! I love curry. It's hot and spicy. Spicy food makes me thirsty. I need to drink a bottle of water when I eat curry. Have you ever eaten curry?

**B** Read the text again. Then choose the correct answer.

1. Monica tells her mom about Ava's e-mail message in her own words. What is she doing?

   ☐ a. paraphrasing      ☐ b. identifying the 5 Ws

2. Ava writes to Monica about who cooks dinner and what she makes. What is she doing?

   ☐ a. paraphrasing      ☐ b. identifying the 5 Ws

**C** Answer the questions and discuss your answers with the class.

1. What could Ava tell her mom about Monica?

2. Who makes the best curry in the world? Why is it so good?

**D** Choose the correct answer.

1. Are Monica and Ava sisters?

☐ a. No, they are cousins.

☐ b. No, they are e-mail pen pals.

☐ c. No, they are classmates.

☐ d. No, they are neighbors.

2. What is Monica's favorite food?

☐ a. cheese

☐ b. noodles

☐ c. curry

☐ d. meatballs

3. What food does Ava love?

☐ a. meatballs

☐ b. noodles

☐ c. curry

☐ d. sushi

4. What does Ava drink when she eats curry?

☐ a. a bottle of water

☐ b. a glass of milk

☐ c. a cup of coffee

☐ d. none of the above

**E** Discuss with a partner.

1. Why do you think Monica and Ava send each other e-mails?

2. What desserts do you like?

3. What other foods would Ava need to drink a bottle of water with?

**F** Choose the correct word.

Monica and Ava are pen pals. They send each other (1. **letters** / **e-mails**) to share information about their lives. They tell each other about their favorite (2. **shoes** / **foods**). Ava tells Monica that her family usually eats (3. **meatballs** / **curry**) for dinner. Spicy food makes Ava (4. **thirsty** / **hungry**). Ava drinks (5. **a glass of milk** / **a bottle of water**) with her spicy dinner and Monica drinks (6. **a glass of milk** / **a bottle of water**) with her dessert.

**WHAT CAN YOU DO?** Color the stars.

I can paraphrase. ★★★

I can identify the 5 Ws in a text. ★★★

KEY

★ I need help.

★★ I can do this a little.

★★★ I can do this well.

# Get Ready to Write

## WRITING GOAL: Write an Explanatory Text

An explanatory text uses information to explain something. It increases readers' knowledge and helps them understand a topic better.

**A** Read the explanatory text. Underline the transitions.

> **Writing Tip**
> Use transitions like *also*, *in fact*, and *as well* to introduce more information.

Topic of explanatory text

### Coffee Beans: From Field to Cup

The coffee your parents drink every day took a long trip to get to your house. In fact, the trip began in a field, maybe in another country, such as Brazil or Colombia.

Information that explains and increases knowledge about the topic

The <u>coffee bean is a seed.</u> Farmers plant the seeds and coffee trees grow. These trees have fruit.

After the fruit is picked, <u>it is dried in the sun</u>. The dry coffee beans are packed in bags and sent around the world.

When the coffee beans arrive in your country, they are <u>roasted in ovens</u>. Local stores sell them to people who like a hot cup of coffee, maybe with some cupcakes, as well. You may prefer a glass of milk and a box of chocolates. Do you know where these come from?

**B** Discuss the questions with a partner.

1. Where do coffee beans come from?
2. What happens after farmers plant coffee beans?
3. How do the coffee beans get to your country?
4. Where do people buy coffee to make a cup of coffee at home?

# Write

**C** Think about a food you would like to know more about. Find information about the food. Complete the chart.

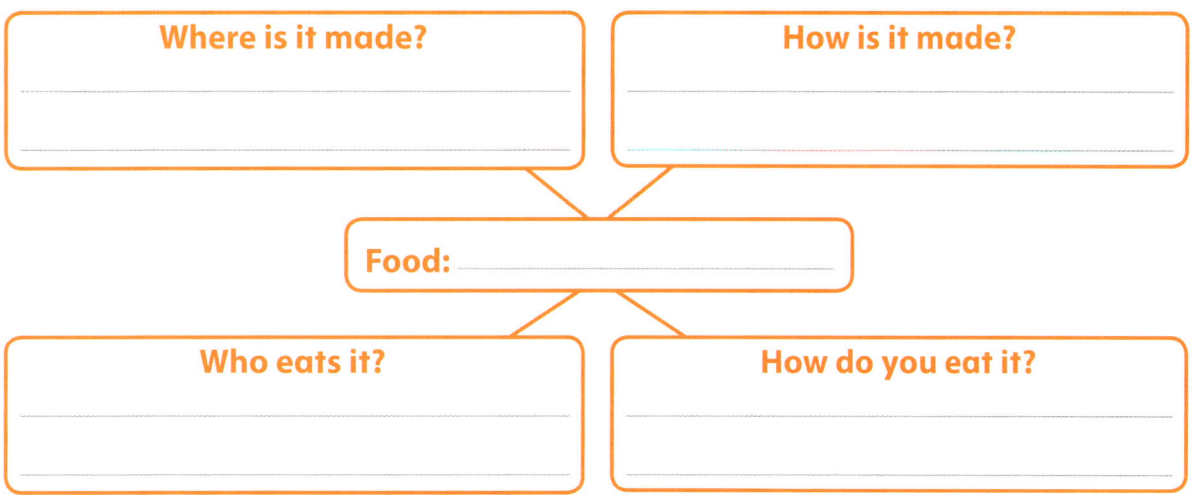

| Where is it made? | How is it made? |

Food:

| Who eats it? | How do you eat it? |

**D** Write about the food you want to know about. Use your information from **C**.
Use new information, too. Remember to use transitions.

1. What food do you want to learn more about?

   _____

2. Where is it made?

   _____

3. How is it made?

   _____

4. Who eats it?

   _____

5. How do you eat it?

   _____

Now write an explanatory text about that food.

**WHAT CAN YOU DO?**  Color the stars.

I can write an explanatory text about a food. ⭐⭐⭐

I can use *also, in fact,* and *as well* to introduce more information. ⭐⭐⭐

**KEY**

⭐ I need help.

⭐⭐ I can do this a little.

⭐⭐⭐ I can do this well.

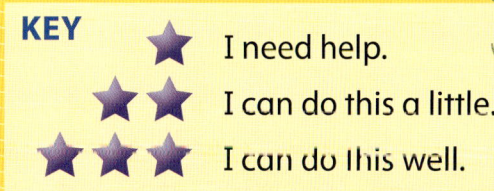

TOPIC

2

SCIENCE

# The Animal Kingdom

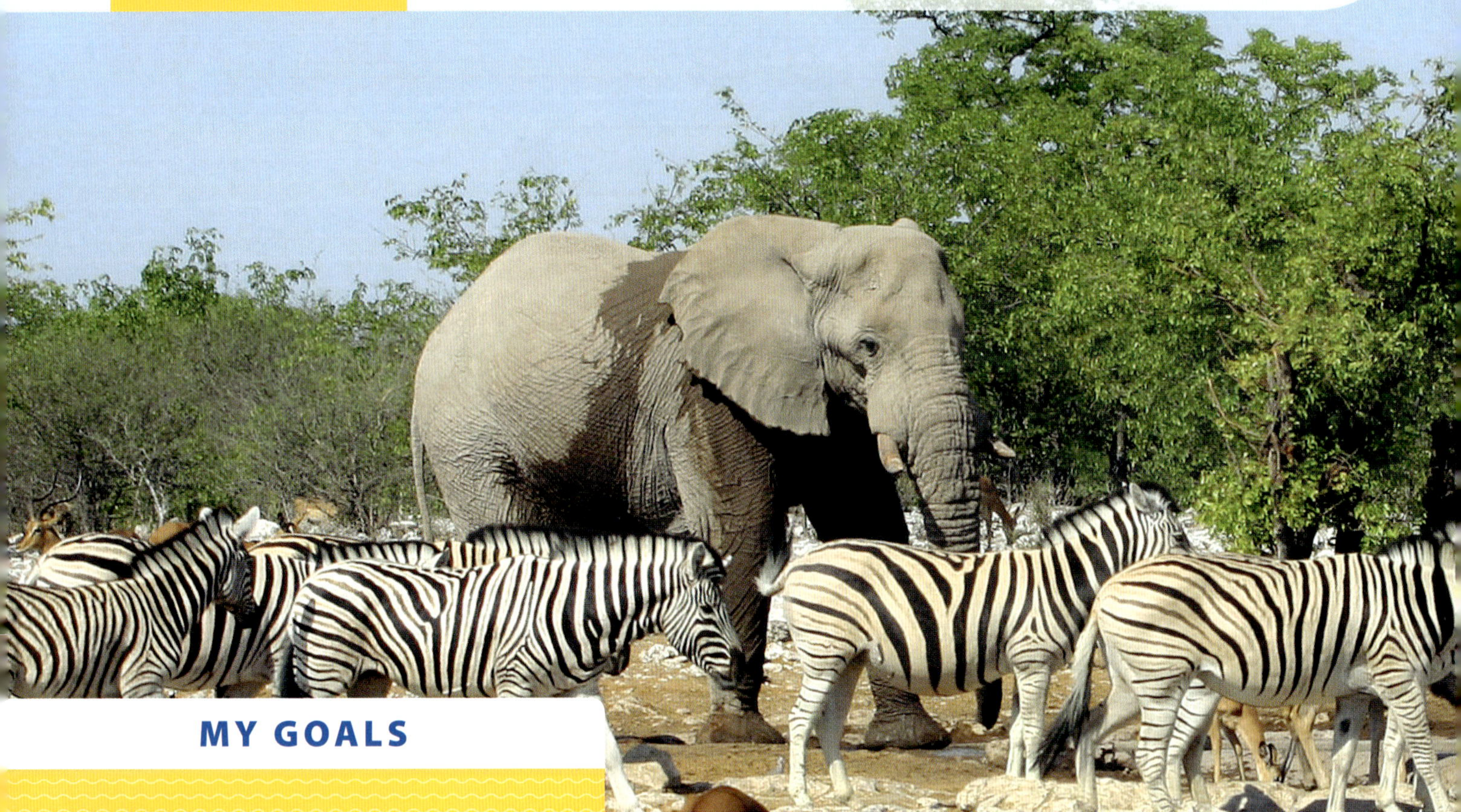

## MY GOALS

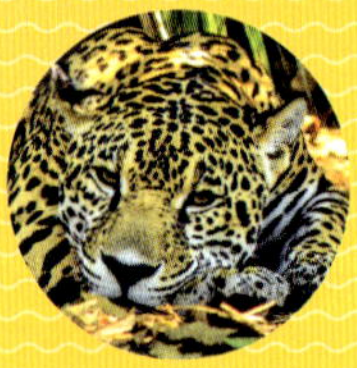

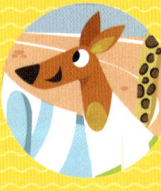

### UNIT 3

- Read the article *Now You See Them, Now You Don't*
- Make connections

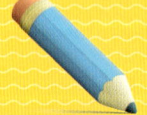

### UNIT 4

- Read the story *The Big Race*
- Classify and categorize

### WRITE

- Write a report

**A** **Look at the picture.**

1. What animals do you see?
2. What is the giraffe doing?

## Animals in Africa

These zebras, elephants, and giraffes live in Africa. Each zebra has a different stripe pattern and each giraffe has a different spot pattern. Did you know the giraffe is the tallest mammal in the world? A baby giraffe is taller than most humans. And giraffes have huge tongues. Some giraffes have tongues that are 45 centimeters long!

**B** **Read the text.**

1. Where do these zebras, elephants, and giraffes live?

2. How tall is a baby giraffe?

3. How are zebras and giraffes alike?

**Think, Pair, Share**
What African animal do you want to see? Why?

# Read

## READING GOAL: Make Connections

We can make connections between a text and our own experiences. When you read, ask, *How is this similar to my life?* Your answers can give you a deeper understanding of the text.

## Get Ready

**A** Read. Choose the answer that makes a connection.

1. The main character in this book has two sisters.

  ☐ a. I have two sisters, too.

  ☐ b. I left my book at home.

2. Ana's favorite author is Alex Bow.

  ☐ a. I don't like comic books.

  ☐ b. I read a book by Alex Bow.

**B** Find the <mark>key words</mark> in the article. Look up the words you don't know in your dictionary.

**C** Read and listen to the article *Now You See Them, Now You Don't*.  5

# Now You See Them, Now You Don't

Animals, large and small, use camouflage to keep them safe. Camouflage is the way an animal hides by blending into, or matching, its background.

## Small Animals

5  <mark>Smaller</mark> animals can blend into their backgrounds easily. For example, squirrels are the same color as trees branches. When a <mark>squirrel</mark> stands still, it blends in with the tree. Some <mark>lizards</mark> rest on plants or rocks that match
10  their color. Other lizards can change color to match their backgrounds!

## Large Animals

Some <mark>larger</mark> animals use camouflage, too.
15  They have fur that helps them hide in nature. The gold fur of a lion is like the color of the dry grasses in Africa where it lives. So lions are hard to see in their environment. Some <mark>jaguars</mark> have gold fur and dark spots. They live in forests where the spotty patterns on their fur help
20  them blend in. <mark>Polar bears</mark> live where it is always cold and snowy. Because of their white fur, polar bears are hard to see in the snow.

## Insects

25 Insects, like <mark>caterpillars</mark> and <mark>butterflies</mark>, also have colors that help them hide. Some caterpillars are green or brown to blend in with tree branches or leaves. Some butterflies have different patterns that help them blend in.

What animals have you seen blend into their environments? **Make connections** with your own experiences.

**Whether an animal is large or small, camouflage is important to keep it safe.**

### WHAT CAN YOU DO?   Color the stars.

I can read the article and make connections with my own experiences. ⭐⭐⭐

I can understand all the key words. ⭐⭐⭐

**KEY**
⭐ I need help.
⭐⭐ I can do this a little.
⭐⭐⭐ I can do this well.

# Understand

**Remember!**
We can **make connections** between a text and our own experiences.

**A**  Think about making connections. Answer the questions and discuss with the class.

1. Animals use camouflage to hide from danger. What are some reasons for you to hide?

2. Have you ever seen people use camouflage? Explain.

3. What experiences have you had that help you make connections with the text?

4. Why is it important to make connections when you read?

**B**  Choose the correct answer.

1. What color are some jaguars?
   - [ ] a. gold with dark spots
   - [ ] b. gold with white spots
   - [ ] c. white with black spots
   - [ ] d. black with white spots

2. Where does a polar bear blend in?
   - [ ] a. in a forest
   - [ ] b. next to a tree
   - [ ] c. in the snow
   - [ ] d. under green leaves

3. What large animals use camouflage to hide in nature?
   - [ ] a. jaguars
   - [ ] b. lions
   - [ ] c. polar bears
   - [ ] d. all of the above

4. What animal can change color to match its background?
   - [ ] a. a squirrel
   - [ ] b. a lizard
   - [ ] c. a lion
   - [ ] d. a polar bear

**C**  Ask and answer the questions with a partner.

1. Why do some animals use camouflage?

2. What other animals use camouflage? Explain how they do it.

3. What are some ways camouflage could help you?

4. What is your favorite animal that uses camouflage? Why?

**D** Complete the sentences.

| smaller | larger | polar bear | squirrel | caterpillar | butterfly | lizard | jaguar |

A (1) _____ has fur the same color as a tree branch. It is (2) _____ than a duck, but (3) _____ than a hamster. You may not see it if it's next to a tree. A (4) _____ can blend in with the snow, and the spotty pattern on a (5) _____ can blend in with the leaves in a forest. A (6) _____ can change color so it blends in with its background. A (7) _____ is an insect that will become a (8) _____. They both blend in with the plants and leaves around them.

**E** Read and complete the sentences with one, two, or three words.

### Lizards Make Great Pets

Have you ever thought about having a lizard for a pet? Lizards make great pets! We are looking for a good home for our pet lizard, Lizzie. She is very easy to take care of. Since she is smaller than a dog, she doesn't eat much. And she is larger than a caterpillar, so she won't get lost in your house, either. Lizzie is friendly, quiet, and graceful. And she can change color! Just be careful. If Lizzie changes color, you may not be able to see her! Call 312-8753 for information.

1. A lizard makes a great _____

2. Lizards are _____ dogs.

3. Lizards are _____ caterpillars.

4. Lizzie is friendly, _____

5. If a lizard changes color from brown to _____ , you might not see it resting on a leaf.

## WHAT CAN YOU DO?  Color the stars.

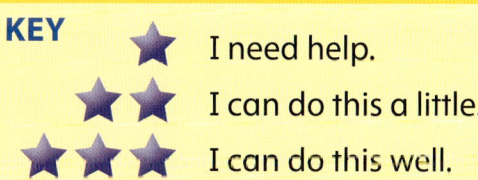

I can make connections between a text and my own experiences to give me a deeper understanding of what I'm reading. ★★★

KEY
★ I need help.
★★ I can do this a little.
★★★ I can do this well.

# Read

**READING GOAL: Classify and Categorize**

To classify, put similar things into a group. To categorize, give the group a name that describes it. When you read, classify and categorize to understand how things are similar and different.

## Get Ready

 **A** **Read and categorize.**

1. Dolphins, fish, and whales
   - ☐ a. water animals
   - ☐ b. land animals

2. Parrots, peacocks, and eagles
   - ☐ a. insects
   - ☐ b. birds

3. Dogs, cats, and hamsters
   - ☐ a. animals that live in the desert
   - ☐ b. animals that make good pets

**B** **Find the key words in the story. Look up the words you don't know in your dictionary.**

**C** **Read and listen to the story *The Big Race*.** 🔊 6

## The Big Race

Today is a bright, sunny day in Petsville. Every year on this day the town gathers for the Big Race. A kangaroo, gazelle, parrot, cheetah, and camel are ready to race.

5 The crowd stands quietly, and everyone wonders. Can the flying parrot beat all the other animals? The kangaroo hops on two legs. Is it faster than the gazelle, cheetah, and camel? They have four
10 legs! The crowd can't wait to find out.

Frog blows the whistle. The parrot flaps its wings and flies off. The kangaroo takes off with a huge hop. The gazelle, cheetah, and camel start to run
15 quickly. Everyone cheers loudly.

Rabbit asks, "Which one is faster, the gazelle or the cheetah?"

"The gazelle is fast, but the cheetah is faster," replies Fox. "The cheetah is the
20 fastest runner with four legs."

"Have you ever seen a dolphin swim?" asks Fox. "Dolphins are very fast in the water without any legs. You don't need legs to be fast!"

START

Can you put the animals into groups that are similar? What name describes each group?

25    "Look!" exclaims Mouse. "The cheetah and the gazelle are crossing the finish line. Next comes the hopping kangaroo. And then the camel finishes slowly on four legs. But where's the parrot? Look! It's flying so far behind the others."

30    Fox replies, "The parrot may be slower than the other animals, but it's the most colorful! Fly, parrot. Fly!"

**WHAT CAN YOU DO?**   Color the stars.

I can understand the story and classify or categorize information in it. ★ ★ ★

I can understand all the key words. ★ ★ ★

KEY

★            I need help.

★ ★        I can do this a little.

★ ★ ★    I can do this well.

# Understand

**A** Think about classifying and categorizing information. Answer the questions and discuss with the class.

1. Which animals run the race?

2. Which two animals win the race? How would you categorize them?

3. What is another category you can make with the information in the story? What animals would you put into that category?

4. How does classifying and categorizing the animals in the story help you?

**B** Read. Choose **T** for **True** and **F** for **False**.

| | | T | F |
|---|---|---|---|
| 1. | The Big Race takes place every year in Petsville. | T | F |
| 2. | No one is there to see the race. | T | F |
| 3. | Frog blows the whistle and the race begins. | T | F |
| 4. | The kangaroo hops the race. | T | F |
| 5. | The parrot and the camel run the race. | T | F |
| 6. | Dolphins and gazelles have four legs. | T | F |
| 7. | The cheetah wins the race. | T | F |
| 8. | The parrot is the slowest animal in the race. | T | F |

**C** Ask and answer the questions with a partner.

1. How is the Big Race different from other races? What kind of races have you been in?

2. What does the crowd talk about while the animals race? Give examples.

3. Is it faster to run or hop the race? How do you know?

4. What is special about the parrot? What other animals do something special?

## D  Choose the correct answer.

1. In line 6, the word *parrot* refers to
   - ☐ a. the fastest animal.
   - ☐ b. a colorful bird.
   - ☐ c. an animal that hops.
   - ☐ d. an animal that swims.

2. In line 7, the word *kangaroo* refers to
   - ☐ a. a colorful bird.
   - ☐ b. a very slow animal.
   - ☐ c. an animal that leaps.
   - ☐ d. an animal that hops.

3. In line 8, the word *faster* means something is
   - ☐ a. moving more quickly than something else.
   - ☐ b. moving more slowly than something else.
   - ☐ c. moving more gracefully than something else.
   - ☐ d. not moving.

4. In line 22, the *dolphin* is described as
   - ☐ a. fast.
   - ☐ b. slow.
   - ☐ c. smart.
   - ☐ d. colorful.

## E  Read the text. Then read the questions and choose the correct answer.

Many animals run, swim, or fly. But my favorite animals hop. A kangaroo hops from one place to another. Rabbits hop, too. Like kangaroos, rabbits have long, strong back legs. They push with their back legs and hop. Grasshoppers use strong back legs to hop, too. Rabbits move from one place to another faster than grasshoppers because they're larger and they have longer legs. But of all these hopping animals, the kangaroo moves the fastest.

1. How are kangaroos, rabbits, and grasshoppers alike?
   - ☐ a. They all swim.
   - ☐ b. They all hop.
   - ☐ c. They all fly.

2. Which animal moves faster than all the others?
   - ☐ a. a grasshopper
   - ☐ b. a rabbit
   - ☐ c. a kangaroo

## WHAT CAN YOU DO?  Color the stars.

I can put similar things into a group to help me organize and remember what I read.
⭐⭐⭐

KEY
⭐ I need help.
⭐⭐ I can do this a little.
⭐⭐⭐ I can do this well.

# Reading Check

**Remember!**
While you read, **make connections** and **classify and categorize** information to help you understand how things are similar and different.

**A** Read and listen to the article. 🔊 7

## Animal Kinds and Characteristics

There are many different kinds of animals in the world.

**Mammals**

Mammals have hair or fur and they breathe air. Mammals include the jaguar, cheetah, kangaroo, and dolphin. Even a dolphin that lives in water is a mammal, because it lifts its head out of the water to breathe air.

**Birds**

All birds have feathers and lay eggs. Some birds are smaller than others. Some birds fly faster than others. There are even birds that do not fly. Some birds, like the parrot, are very colorful. Others are brown and blend into their environments.

**Insects**

Butterflies and caterpillars are insects. Like all insects, they have three body sections. Caterpillars eat leaves and grow quickly. One day, the caterpillar will turn into a butterfly.

**B** Read the text again. Then choose the correct answer.

1. You want to sort animals by their characteristics. What should you do?

   ☐ a. make connections          ☐ b. classify and categorize

2. You know mammals have hair and breathe air. Humans have hair and breathe air, too. What are you doing?

   ☐ a. making connections        ☐ b. classifying and categorizing

**C** Answer the questions and discuss your answers with the class.

1. What kinds of animals do you have in your environment?

2. Have you been to a zoo? What types of animals did you see there?

**D** Choose the correct answer.

1. Which of these animals are mammals?
   - ☐ a. cheetahs
   - ☐ b. kangaroos
   - ☐ c. jaguars
   - ☐ d. all of the above

2. Why is a dolphin a mammal and not a fish?
   - ☐ a. It swims in the water.
   - ☐ b. It breathes air.
   - ☐ c. It has feathers.
   - ☐ d. It eats insects.

3. How are all birds alike?
   - ☐ a. They all have feathers.
   - ☐ b. They can all fly.
   - ☐ c. They are all very colorful.
   - ☐ d. They all have fur.

4. How are all insects alike?
   - ☐ a. They all fly.
   - ☐ b. They all eat meat.
   - ☐ c. They all have three body parts.
   - ☐ d. They all swim.

**E** Discuss with a partner.

1. Can mammals live underwater?

2. Why is it easy for some brown birds to blend into their environments?

**F** Choose the best word.

Dear Ricky,

In science class, we learned about different groups of animals, like mammals, (1. **parrots** / **birds**), and insects. My favorite mammal is a (2. **cheetah** / **caterpillar**). It's the (3. **slowest** / **fastest**) animal and has spots that help it (4. **hide** / **run**). My favorite bird is a (5. **parrot** / **kangaroo**) because it is very colorful. Some (6. **lizards** / **butterflies**) are very colorful. Here is a picture of these beautiful (7. **insects** / **mammals**). What's your favorite bird?

Angela

**WHAT CAN YOU DO?** Color the stars.

I can make connections.  ★ ★ ★

I can classify and categorize. ★ ★ ★

**KEY**
★ I need help.
★ ★ I can do this a little.
★ ★ ★ I can do this well.

# Get Ready to Write

## WRITING GOAL: Write a Report

A report includes information you learned about a topic. When you write a report, include an introduction, facts and details, a picture with a caption, and a conclusion.

**A** Read the report. Underline the headings.

> **Writing Tip**
> Use headings to organize information in your report.

### DOLPHINS

**Introduction** — A dolphin is a mammal that lives in the sea. It lifts its head out of the water to breathe air.

**What they look like**

Dolphins are gray, so they blend in with ocean water. Smaller dolphins are about a meter long. Larger dolphins can grow as long as 7 meters.

**How they move**

**Facts and details** — Dolphins are not the fastest creatures in the sea — sharks are much faster — but dolphins swim quickly and can jump out of the water.

Dolphins are very friendly.

**Caption**

**What they are like**

Dolphins are very friendly to each other and to humans. Scientists believe they may be the smartest animals in the sea.

**Conclusion** — If you want to see dolphins, walk along the beach. You may see them playing together or jumping in the sea.

**B** Discuss the questions with a partner.

1. What does a dolphin look like?

2. How do dolphins move?

3. Are dolphins the fastest creatures in the sea?

4. What are two other facts about dolphins?

# Write

**C**  Choose an animal. Use headings to organize the information. Fill in the chart.

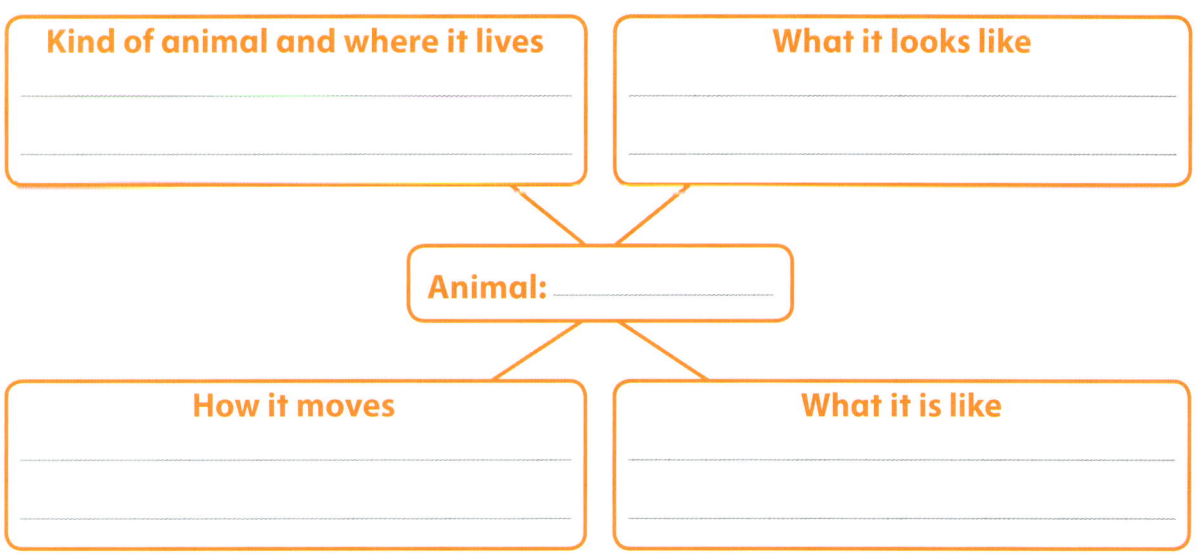

| Kind of animal and where it lives | What it looks like |
|---|---|

**Animal:** _____

| How it moves | What it is like |
|---|---|

**D**  Write about your animal. Use your words from **C** . Choose new words, too.

1. What kind of animal is it? Explain how you know.

   _____

2. Where does it live?

   _____

3. What does it look like?

   _____

4. How does it move?

   _____

5. What is it like?

   _____

Now write a report about your animal.

**WHAT CAN YOU DO?**   Color the stars.

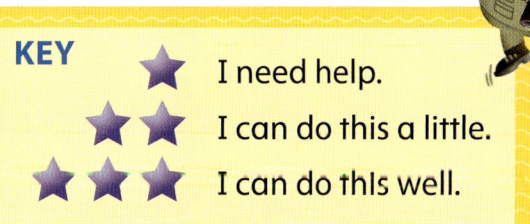

I can write a report about an animal.
⭐⭐⭐

I can use headings to organize information.
⭐⭐⭐

**KEY**

⭐ I need help.

⭐⭐ I can do this a little.

⭐⭐⭐ I can do this well.

# TOPIC 3
# SOCIAL STUDIES

# Around the House

## MY GOALS

### UNIT 5

- Read the story *Daniel Learns a Lesson*
- Identify the theme

### UNIT 6

- Read the magazine article *Visiting an Ice Hotel*
- Identify cause and effect

### WRITE

- Write an essay

**A** Look at the picture.

1. What do you see? What is happening?

2. How does the robot look like a person? How does it look different?

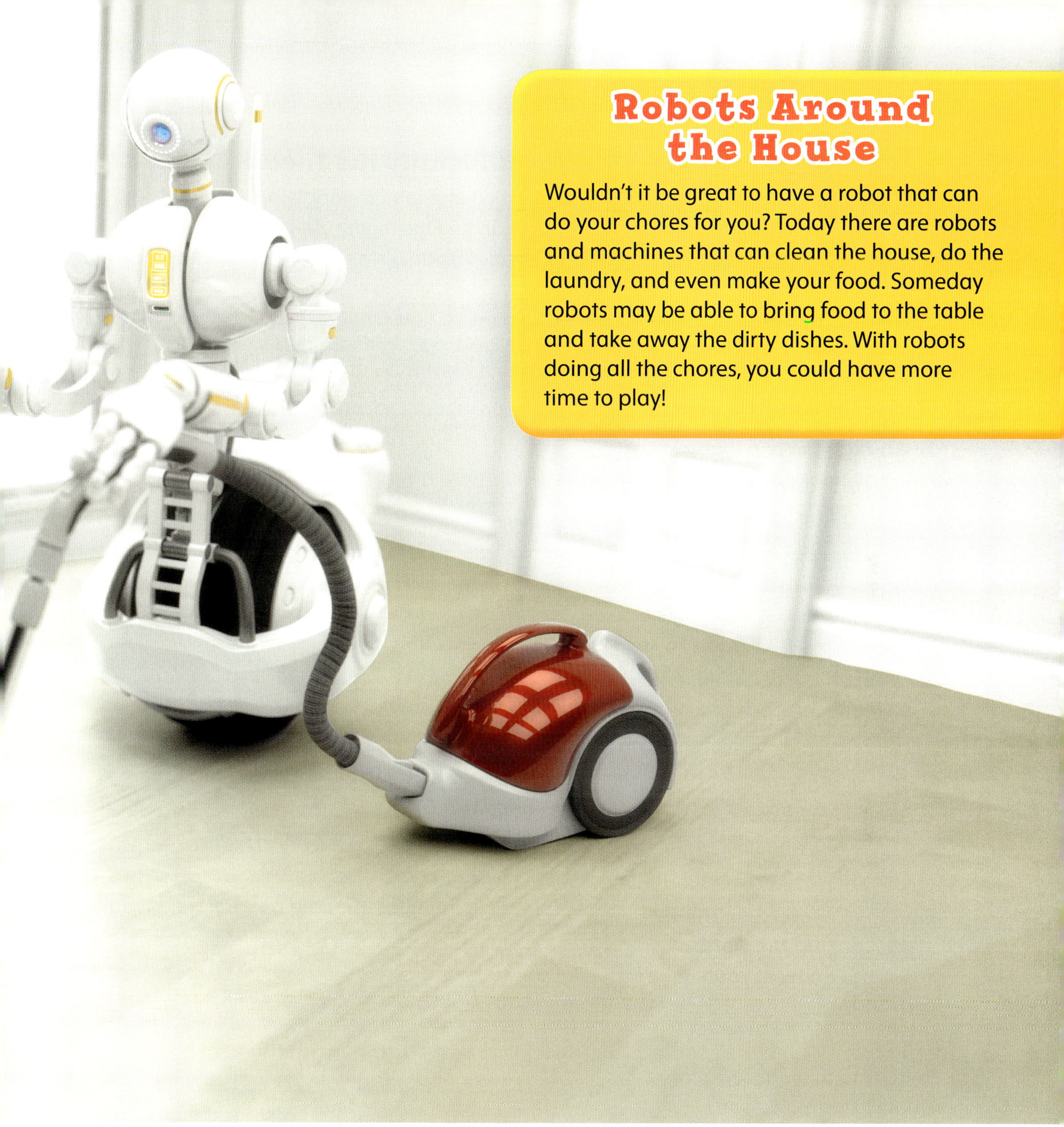

## Robots Around the House

Wouldn't it be great to have a robot that can do your chores for you? Today there are robots and machines that can clean the house, do the laundry, and even make your food. Someday robots may be able to bring food to the table and take away the dirty dishes. With robots doing all the chores, you could have more time to play!

**B** **Read the text.**

1. What can some robots do?
2. What can robots do with dishes?
3. How can robots make your life better?

**Think, Pair, Share**
What chores would you like a robot to do for you?

# Read

**READING GOAL: Identify the Theme**

A theme is a lesson you can learn from a story. Usually, the writer doesn't tell the reader the theme. To find the theme after you read, ask, *What did the character learn? What did I learn?*

## Get Ready

**A** Choose the correct answer.

1. An example of a theme is:
   - ☐ a. Sharing with your friends is important.
   - ☐ b. In the future, robots will do work around the house.

2. An example of a theme is:
   - ☐ a. Billy and Robin like to play volleyball on the weekend.
   - ☐ b. Never give up on yourself.

**B** Find the <mark>key words</mark> in the story. Look up the words you don't know in your dictionary.

**C** Read and listen to the story *Daniel Learns a Lesson*.
 8

# Daniel Learns a Lesson

Every weekday, Daniel and his brother Evan do chores to <mark>help their parents</mark>. Daniel <mark>sets the alarm</mark> and gets up early to <mark>walk the dog</mark>. His dog, Shadow, loves to take long walks in the cool morning air. They walk to the park near their house.

Evan helps their mom in the kitchen. He <mark>sets the table</mark> while their mom <mark>cooks</mark> breakfast. During the week, they usually have toast or cereal with a glass of milk for breakfast. Then Evan <mark>washes the dishes</mark> and they go to school.

On the weekends, Daniel and his brother have even more chores to do. Daniel has to walk the dog and <mark>cut the grass</mark>. Evan has to <mark>wash the car</mark>.

5

10

15  Both Evan and Daniel do these chores happily because they know that when all the chores are done for the week, the family goes on an adventure and has fun together. Last week, they took a boat ride, and this week, they're planning to go to the zoo.

20  But this week, Daniel played with his friends and didn't do his chores. On Sunday, Daniel woke up excited to go to the zoo with his family. He put on his favorite shirt and got in the car with his brother. That's when his dad told him he couldn't go to the zoo this week because he didn't help.

25  Instead of going on an adventure, Daniel had to stay home and do his chores. He was very sad. While he was at home, he promised to always do his chores and never miss another family adventure.

Ask yourself, *What did the character learn?* to find the **theme**.

## WHAT CAN YOU DO?   Color the stars.

I can read the story and identify the theme.
⭐⭐⭐

I can understand all the key words.
⭐⭐⭐

**KEY**

⭐  I need help.

⭐⭐  I can do this a little.

⭐⭐⭐  I can do this well.

# Understand

**A** Think about the theme. Answer the questions and discuss with the class.

1. Who are Daniel and Evan helping by doing chores?

2. Why do they do the chores happily on weekends?

3. Do they enjoy their adventures together?

4. What does Daniel learn about helping his parents at home?

**B** Choose the correct answer.

1. What does Daniel do every morning?
   - ☐ a. walks the dog
   - ☐ b. washes the car
   - ☐ c. cuts the grass
   - ☐ d. cooks breakfast

2. What does his brother do while Daniel walks the dog?
   - ☐ a. washes the car
   - ☐ b. makes breakfast
   - ☐ c. sets the table
   - ☐ d. cuts the grass

3. What does the family eat for breakfast on weekdays?
   - ☐ a. fruit
   - ☐ b. rice
   - ☐ c. pancakes
   - ☐ d. cereal

4. What chore does Daniel do on weekends?
   - ☐ a. sets the table
   - ☐ b. cuts the grass
   - ☐ c. cooks dinner
   - ☐ d. washes the dishes

**C** Ask and answer the questions with a partner.

1. When do Daniel and Evan do their chores on school days?

2. What does his mom do while Daniel walks the dog?

3. Why can't Daniel go to the zoo?

4. What adventures would you like to experience for doing chores?

**D** Complete the sentences.

> set the alarm    wash the car    set the table    wash the dishes
>
> cut the grass    help my parents    walk the dog    cook

My family is going to the country for a few days. Tomorrow we will

(1) _____ and get up early. Our dog, Daisy, will come

with us. Before we go, I will have to (2) _____. Dad will

(3) _____ some food for the trip and then I will clean up the

kitchen and (4) _____. While we are away, our neighbor will

(5) _____ and water the plants.

When we arrive at the lake, we will have a picnic. I will take out the plates and

(6) _____ for lunch. Dad will serve the food. At night, I will

(7) _____ set up a tent. Then, when we get home, I will have

to (8) _____ if it is dirty from the trip.

**E** Read and complete the sentences with one, two, or three words.

### A Job Well Done

Sophia likes to help her parents around the house, but not when she has a soccer game. Today, was the big game. So she cut the grass quickly and left the cut grass in a pile in the yard. "I'll clean up later," she told herself.

Sophia's team won. She was happy … until she got home. The wind blew the grass everywhere! Now, she had to clean it up. "I wish I hadn't left the grass in the yard," she cried.

1. *It is better to do things right the first time* is the _____ of this story.

2. It is Sophia's job to _____

3. The _____ blew the grass everywhere.

4. Sophia had to _____ the grass when she got home.

## WHAT CAN YOU DO?   Color the stars.

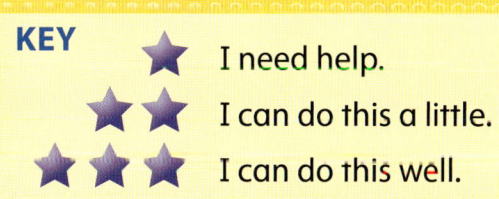

I can identify the theme to learn a lesson from the story. ★ ★ ★

**KEY**

★ I need help.

★ ★ I can do this a little.

★ ★ ★ I can do this well.

# Read

**READING GOAL: Identify Cause and Effect**

A cause is why something happens. An effect is what happens because of a cause. A cause can have many effects. When you read, identify causes and effects to understand how events are related.

## Get Ready

**A** Read the sentences below. Choose the correct answer.

1. It started to rain. Some people opened their umbrellas. Other people put on rain hats.

   ☐ a. The first sentence is a cause.

   ☐ b. The second and third sentences are causes.

2. Kara missed the bus. She had to ride her bike to school, and she was late for her first class.

   ☐ a. The first sentence is an effect.

   ☐ b. The second and third sentences are effects.

**B** Find the key words in the magazine article. Look up the words you don't know in your dictionary.

**C** Read and listen to the magazine article *Visiting an Ice Hotel.* 🔊 9

The Icehotel in Sweden is not like other hotels. This hotel is built from ice and snow from a nearby river. Beds, chairs, and tables are all made from blocks of ice. Guests sleep in special
5   sleeping bags. The floors are made of snow.

Because the hotel is made of ice, people who work there don't have the same jobs as workers in other hotels, and the cooking has to be done in another building.

10   When hotel workers clean up your room, they don't mop the floor because it's made of snow. They don't clean the desk or dust the furniture because there is no dust on ice. They don't make the bed because it's a sleeping bag. And they
15   don't wash the windows because there are no windows, just thick walls of ice.

Only the people who work in the kitchen do normal jobs. They buy groceries, put away the groceries, and cook meals.

20 The hotel is open from December through April. In April, the weather warms up. The hotel melts and visitors go north to look for snow. In December, when the river freezes again, a new ice hotel is built, and new visitors come.

When the weather warms up, it causes two things to happen. What are they? Can you understand how **the cause and the effects** are related?

## WHAT CAN YOU DO?  Color the stars.

I can read the article and understand cause and effect. ★ ★ ★

I can understand all the key words.
★ ★ ★

KEY

★ I need help.

★ ★ I can do this a little.

★ ★ ★ I can do this well.

# Understand

**Remember!**
A cause can have many effects. When you read, identify the **cause and effects** to understand how events are related.

**A** Think about cause and effect. Answer the questions and discuss with the class.

1. What two things happen because the hotel is made of ice?

2. Why don't the workers in the Icehotel clean the desks or dust the furniture?

3. What happens when the river freezes again in December?

4. Why is it important to identify cause and effect when you read?

**B** Read. Choose **T** for **True** and **F** for **False**.

| | | |
|---|---|---|
| 1. The Icehotel is made of ice and snow. | T | F |
| 2. All the furniture in the hotel is wood. | T | F |
| 3. The ice rooms are warm. | T | F |
| 4. The people who work at the hotel wash the windows every week. | T | F |
| 5. The hotel kitchen is made of ice. | T | F |
| 6. When the hotel melts, visitors go swimming in the river. | T | F |
| 7. In April, the hotel melts. | T | F |
| 8. The river freezes again in September. | T | F |

**C** Ask and answer the questions with a partner.

1. The Icehotel is made from ice and snow. Where do they get the snow and ice?

2. Where do people sleep in the Icehotel to stay warm?

3. Why do you think people can't cook in a room made of ice?

4. Why is working in the Icehotel different from working in other hotels?

## D  Choose the correct answer.

1. In line 10, *clean up your room* means
   - ☐ a. put away your clothes, and make the bed.
   - ☐ b. put the groceries in the refrigerator.
   - ☐ c. get food at the supermarket.
   - ☐ d. clean the windows.

2. In line 13, *make the bed* means
   - ☐ a. put away your clothes.
   - ☐ b. wash the dishes.
   - ☐ c. get food at the supermarket.
   - ☐ d. tidy the sheets and blankets.

3. In line 15, *wash the windows* means about the same as
   - ☐ a. open the windows.
   - ☐ b. close the windows.
   - ☐ c. clean the windows.
   - ☐ d. wash the floor.

4. In line 18, *buy groceries* means
   - ☐ a. make the bed.
   - ☐ b. get food at the supermarket.
   - ☐ c. clean the windows.
   - ☐ d. put your books and papers in order.

## E  Read the text. Then read the questions and choose the correct answer.

Dear Aunt Ellie,

Mom and I used to go to the supermarket every week to buy groceries. Then we would go to visit Grandma. Since Mom broke her leg, we have to shop online and talk to Grandma on the phone.

Have you tried shopping online? It's so easy! A truck delivers the groceries to our home. You should try it, too!

Jess

1. Because Mom broke her leg, they
   - ☐ a. see Grandma more often.
   - ☐ b. shop online and call Grandma.
   - ☐ c. go to the store.
   - ☐ d. drive a truck.

2. What does Jess think she should try?
   - ☐ a. calling Grandma
   - ☐ b. online shopping
   - ☐ c. going to the supermarket
   - ☐ d. driving a truck

## WHAT CAN YOU DO?  Color the stars.

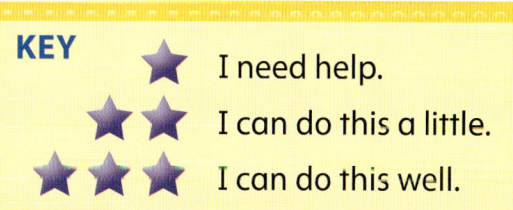

I can identify cause and effect to understand how events are related. ★ ★ ★

KEY  ★  I need help.
     ★ ★  I can do this a little.
     ★ ★ ★  I can do this well.

# Reading Check

**Remember!**
Identify **cause and effect** while you read to help you understand how events are related and then identify the **theme** after you read.

**A** Read and listen.  10

## Robots Make Life Easier

Our teacher divided the class into three teams and asked each to make a robot that does chores. So each team is working together to draw a robot and then build the robot in their drawing.

Team 1 is making a robot to walk the dog and cut the grass.
Team 2's robot will buy groceries and put away the groceries.
My team, Team 3, is making a robot to set the alarm and make the bed.

We share ideas. Our robot's head is an alarm clock that rings. It has wheels so it can roll up beside our bed. It moves its arms to shake us awake and make the bed while we brush our teeth.

Our drawing is amazing!
The robot we make together will be even better!

**B** Read the text again. Then choose the correct answer.

1. You learn that by working together the team can make a great robot. What are you doing?

   ☐ a. identifying the theme          ☐ b. identifying cause and effect

2. The teacher asks each team to make a robot, so they work together to draw the robot and then build it. You underline this because you are

   ☐ a. identifying the theme.          ☐ b. identifying cause and effect.

**C** Answer the questions and discuss your answers with the class.

1. What happens when the robot moves its arms?

2. What lesson did you learn from this story?

**D** Complete the sentences.

1. The teacher asked the class to make robots that _____

   ☐ a. walk.

   ☐ b. talk.

   ☐ c. do chores.

   ☐ d. sing.

3. Team 3's robot has _____ for a head.

   ☐ a. a box

   ☐ b. an alarm clock

   ☐ c. an egg

   ☐ d. a ball

2. First, each team _____ to show what their robot looks like.

   ☐ a. draws a picture

   ☐ b. takes a photograph

   ☐ c. tells a story

   ☐ d. surfs the Internet

4. The robot _____ while the child brushes his teeth.

   ☐ a. sets the table

   ☐ b. cuts the grass

   ☐ c. washes the car

   ☐ d. makes the bed

**E** Discuss with a partner.

1. How do robots make people's lives easier?

2. What would you like a robot to do for you?

**F** Choose the best word.

Everybody has some chores to do around the house. In the house, I have to (1. **clean up my room / wash the car**). First, I (2. **walk the dog / make the bed**). Then sometimes I (3. **dust the furniture / wash the car**). I also (4. **help my parents / make my bed**) outside in the garden. First, I (5. **wash the dishes / cut the grass**). Then I (6. **walk the dog / cook**). There are always lots of (7. **games / chores**) to do around the house.

**WHAT CAN YOU DO?** Color the stars.

I can identify the theme. ⭐⭐⭐

I can identify cause and effect. ⭐⭐⭐

KEY

⭐ I need help.

⭐⭐ I can do this a little.

⭐⭐⭐ I can do this well.

# Get Ready to Write

**WRITING GOAL: Write an Essay**

An essay is a piece of writing about a subject. It includes a title, an interesting introduction with your main idea, body paragraphs that support the main idea, and a conclusion that summarizes the key points.

**A** Read the essay. Underline the phrase that begins the conclusion.

> **Writing Tip**
> To begin your conclusion, use phrases such as *in conclusion* and *to sum it up*.

## Helling Out at Home   by Mateo Martin

**Introduction with main idea**

My sister, Lucy, and I help my parents around the house by doing different chores. My favorite job is to walk the dog. I put on Ruby's leash and we walk to the park every morning after breakfast. I especially like walking Ruby on bright, sunny mornings.

**Body paragraphs that support the main idea**

During the week, Lucy and I take turns setting the table for dinner and washing the dishes. I wash the dishes on Monday, Wednesday, and Friday. She washes them on Tuesday and Thursday, when I set the table.

On Saturdays, Lucy helps my dad cut the grass. My mom and I buy groceries and then we put them away.

**Mateo walking Ruby**

**Conclusion that summarizes key points**

In conclusion, we all do something to help keep our house in order. Our family is happy to work together to get the chores done.

**B** Discuss the questions with a partner.

1. What chores does Mateo do during the week?

2. Which chore does Mateo enjoy the most?

3. What is the main idea of the text?

4. How do Mateo and Lucy feel about helping their parents around the house?

# Write

**C** Think about the chores that you do at home each week. Complete the chart.

**Day**

| | | | |
|---|---|---|---|

**Chores**

**D** Write about the chores that you do at home each week. Use your words from **C**. Choose new words, too.

1. What chores do you do during the week?

   _____

2. What chores do you do on weekends?

   _____

3. What chores do you like to do the most?

   _____

4. Which chore is your least favorite?

   _____

5. How do you feel about doing chores at home?

   _____

✏️ **Now write an essay about your chores.**

**WHAT CAN YOU DO?**  Color the stars.

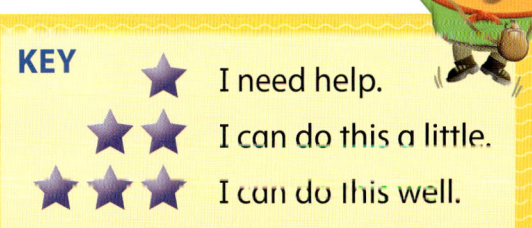

I can write an essay about the chores I do around the house. ⭐⭐⭐

I can use a phrase such as *in conclusion* to begin my conclusion. ⭐⭐⭐

**KEY**
⭐ I need help.
⭐⭐ I can do this a little.
⭐⭐⭐ I can do this well.

TOPIC 4

SCIENCE

# The Four Seasons

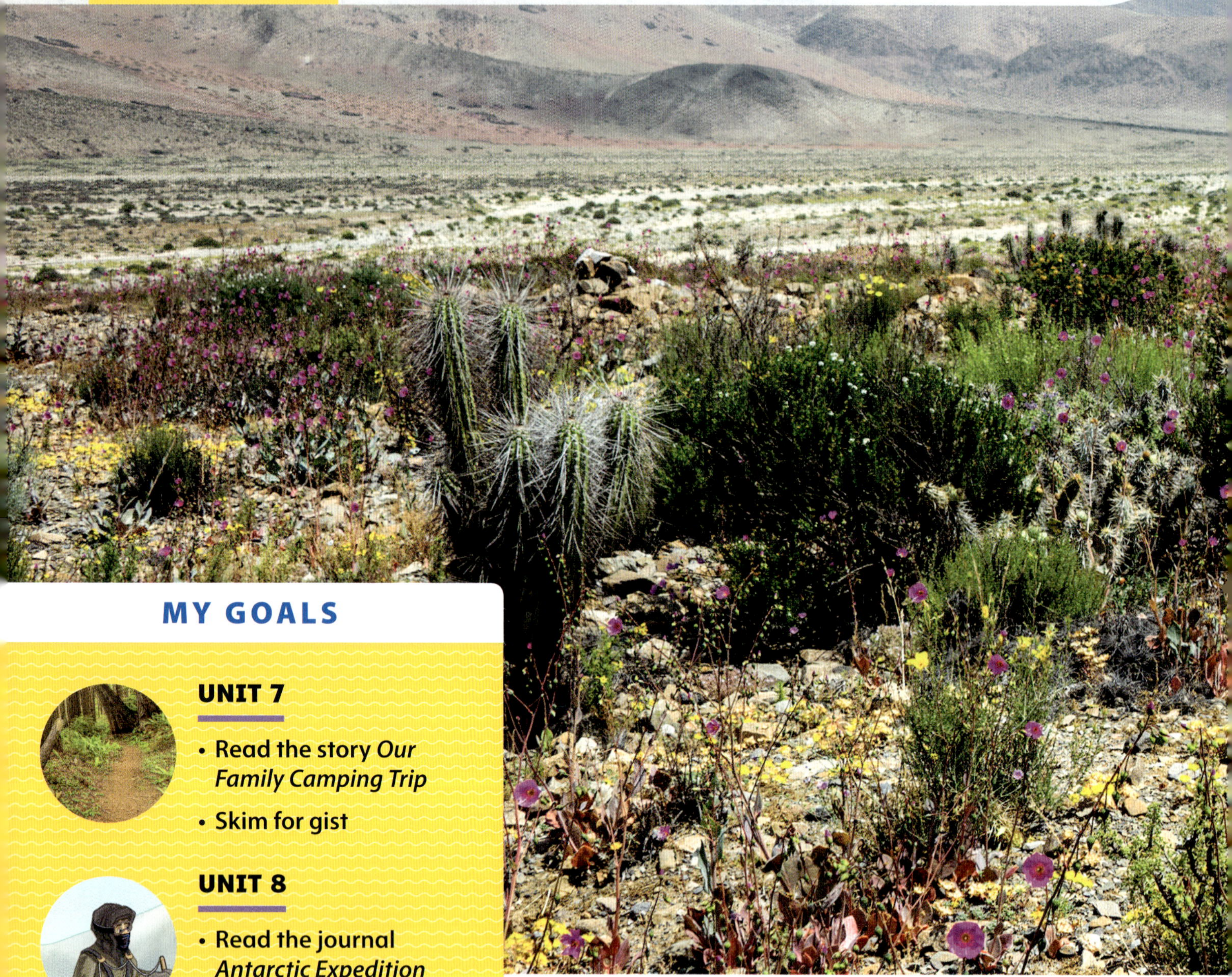

## MY GOALS

**UNIT 7**

- Read the story *Our Family Camping Trip*
- Skim for gist

**UNIT 8**

- Read the journal *Antarctic Expedition*
- Draw conclusions

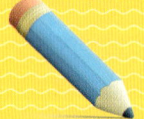

**WRITE**

- Write an opinion essay

**A** **Look at the picture.**

1. What do you see?
2. How is this place similar to or different than where you live?

There are areas in the park where you can set up your tent, or you can stay in a small house made of wood.
15  After a night of camping under the stars, we will get up early and <mark>climb a mountain</mark>.

There are many trails in the mountains. At the highest point, these mountains are almost 1,500 meters high. From the trails, you can see an amazing canyon. We
20  will pack sandwiches and when we reach the rest area, we will <mark>have a picnic</mark>.

It's a great time to sit down and relax before going back down the mountain. It's also important to drink a lot of water and eat to have energy.

25  Hopefully, there was enough rain last <mark>spring</mark> so we can <mark>canoe on the river</mark>, too! If not, there are so many trails to hike, we'll be busy the whole vacation!

What is the **gist** of this story? Underline the words that tell you.

**WHAT CAN YOU DO?**  Color the stars.

I can read the essay and skim for gist. ★ ★ ★
I can understand all the key words. ★ ★ ★

KEY  ★ I need help.
★ ★ I can do this a little.
★ ★ ★ I can do this well.

# Understand

**A** Think about skimming for gist. Answer the questions and discuss with the class.

1. What does the title tell you the essay will be about?

2. Skim the first sentence in the first paragraph. What do you learn?

3. Skim the last sentence in the first paragraph. What do you learn?

4. What do you see in the picture?

**B** Choose the correct answer.

1. Where did the family go on vacation last summer?
   - [ ] a. the beach
   - [ ] b. a zoo
   - [ ] c. camping
   - [ ] d. an amusement park

2. Where will they go this summer?
   - [ ] a. the beach
   - [ ] b. camping
   - [ ] c. a zoo
   - [ ] d. an amusement park

3. What will they do on Stream Trail?
   - [ ] a. canoe on the river
   - [ ] b. climb a mountain
   - [ ] c. go hiking
   - [ ] d. go swimming

4. How high is the highest point in the mountains?
   - [ ] a. 500 meters
   - [ ] b. 1,000 meters
   - [ ] c. 1,500 meters
   - [ ] d. 2,000 meters

**C** Ask and answer the questions with a partner.

1. What can the family do in the state park?

2. Would you prefer a vacation at the Stream Trail or the beach? Explain.

3. What would you do on your dream vacation?

4. Where do people go for vacation in your country?

**D**  Complete the sentences.

> go to the beach    spring    summer    have a picnic
>
> canoe on the river    climb a mountain    go hiking    go camping

Every (1) _____ after the school year ends, we go on vacation.

Sometimes we pack up our bathing suits and towels and (2) _____ .

Other times, we pack up our tent and our sleeping bags and (3) _____ .

There are a lot of fun things to do on a camping trip. You can (4) _____

on a trail or (5) _____ to see a deep canyon. If there is a deep river,

you can (6) _____ .

(7) _____ is the best season to pack a lunch and

(8) _____ because it isn't hot yet. A trip with the family is always a lot of fun!

**E**  Read the article and complete the sentences with one, two, or three words.

### Come Visit Tsavo West National Park

Tsavo West National Park is in Kenya. It is easy to reach by air and by road. The park has 7,000 square kilometers of land where cheetahs, elephants, giraffes, lions, and zebras live. Climb a mountain, then look down and see the animals running wild. The park is open all year round. It rains a lot in spring, so the best time to visit is in summer.

1. By looking at the title, I know this travel article is about Tsavo West
   _____ in Kenya.

2. The park has _____ of land.

3. Cheetahs, elephants, giraffes, lions, and _____ live in the park.

4. It rains a lot in _____

5. The best time to visit is in _____

**WHAT CAN YOU DO?**  Color the stars.

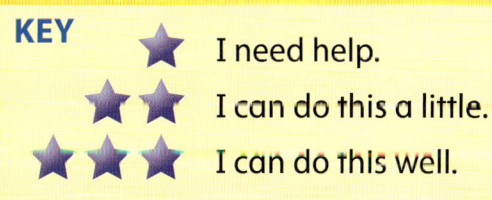

I can skim for gist to learn what the text is about. ⭐⭐⭐

KEY
⭐ I need help.
⭐⭐ I can do this a little.
⭐⭐⭐ I can do this well.

# Read

## READING GOAL: Draw Conclusions

Drawing a conclusion is what you do after thinking carefully about a text. When you read, use words and pictures in a text and your own knowledge to draw conclusions about what the writer doesn't tell you.

## Get Ready

**A** Read the sentences below. Choose the correct conclusion.

1. A boy is wearing a raincoat and using an umbrella.

   ☐ a. It's raining outside.

   ☐ b. It's hot outside.

2. There are a swimsuit, a towel, and goggles in Dani's bag.

   ☐ a. She is a soccer player.

   ☐ b. She is a swimmer.

**B** Find the key words in the journal. Look up the words you don't know in your dictionary.

**C** Read and listen to the journal *Antarctic Expedition.* 🔊 12

# Antarctic Expedition

## 1901

Captain Scott and I, Ernest Shackleton, are on an expedition to explore Antarctica, the most southern point on the Earth. Our ship *Discovery* got to the coast this fall. We will try
5 to get to the South Pole with dogs and sleds. We are wearing heavy coats, boots, hats, and gloves.

## 1902

10 It is winter and everything is covered with snow and ice. Today there was another blizzard. The dogs pulling our sleds are tired and sick. They can't work anymore. We are tired and sick, too, but we have to go on.

15 At night, I dream we could ice skate on the frozen lakes or go skiing on the snowy land. I imagine us sitting by a warm fire and drinking hot chocolate. But during the day, I am afraid we will freeze or run out of food.
20 Soon we will have to return home.

## 1911

Today, the dream Captain Scott had of being the first explorer to reach the South Pole was crushed. A Norwegian man named Roald
25 Amundsen and his team just got there.

## 1915

I wanted to cross Antarctica, but our ship *Endurance* got stuck in ice. Some of us sailed in a lifeboat to get help. Now we need to rescue the others.

Look at the picture of the explorers. What **conclusions** can you draw about their difficult expedition?

**WHAT CAN YOU DO?**   Color the stars.

I can read the journal and draw conclusions.
⭐⭐⭐

I can understand all the key words.
⭐⭐⭐

**KEY**

⭐ I need help.

⭐⭐ I can do this a little.

⭐⭐⭐ I can do this well.

# Understand

**Remember!**
Use words, pictures, and your own knowledge to **draw conclusions** about things the writer doesn't tell you.

**A** Think about drawing conclusions. Answer the questions and discuss with the class.

1. Scott and his men were wearing heavy coats, boots, hats, and gloves. What conclusion can you draw?

2. The explorer says he's afraid they will run out of food or freeze. What conclusions can you draw?

3. How did the men go on when the dogs were too tired and sick to pull the sleds?

4. Why is it important to draw conclusions when you read?

**B** Read. Choose **T** for **True** and **F** for **False**.

1. Captain Scott went on an expedition to the North Pole.             **T**     **F**

2. The *Discovery* got to the coast of Antarctica in the fall of 1901.     **T**     **F**

3. The explorers wore heavy coats, boots, hats, and gloves.             **T**     **F**

4. The explorers used skis to get to the South Pole.             **T**     **F**

5. There are rainstorms but no blizzards in Antarctica.             **T**     **F**

6. The explorers went ice skating and drank hot chocolate.             **T**     **F**

7. Roald Amundsen was the first explorer to reach the South Pole.     **T**     **F**

8. In 1915, the explorer's ship *Endurance* got stuck in ice.             **T**     **F**

**C** Ask and answer the questions with a partner.

1. Why do explorers write journals?

2. Why does this explorer imagine he is drinking hot chocolate?

3. Why was the explorer's dream crushed?

4. Where would you like to explore?

C  Answ

1.  W

2.  W

D  Comp

1.  Fo
    ar

3.  Th

E  Discu

1.  Ha

2.  Wh

F  Choos

In J
of N
colo
and
peop
It is
(6. **h**

**D**  **Choose the correct answer.**

1.  In line 3, *explore* means to
    - [ ] a.  go to an amusement park.
    - [ ] b.  go to a place you know nothing about.
    - [ ] c.  go skiing.
    - [ ] d.  go ice skating.

2.  In line 5, what does *fall* refer to?
    - [ ] a.  what snow and rain do
    - [ ] b.  the season before summer
    - [ ] c.  the season after summer
    - [ ] d.  the season before spring

3.  In line 12, *blizzard* means
    - [ ] a.  strong winds.
    - [ ] b.  a lot of rain.
    - [ ] c.  a person made of snow.
    - [ ] d.  a snowstorm with strong winds.

4.  In line 19, *freeze* means to
    - [ ] a.  feel extremely cold.
    - [ ] b.  feel extremely hot.
    - [ ] c.  feel extremely tired.
    - [ ] d.  feel extremely thirsty.

**E**  **Read the text. Then read the questions and choose the correct answer.**

Dear Leila,

Over winter break, my family went skiing in the Alps. There was a blizzard right before we arrived. The mountains were beautiful.

Joey and I went skiing and I fell in the snow. I was so cold. I thought my nose and fingers would freeze. After skiing, we went into the ski lodge to drink hot chocolate. It was delicious and warm after so much cold weather.

Sincerely,

Olivia

1.  Olivia said there was a blizzard right before they arrived. What conclusion can you draw?
    - [ ] a.  It was snowing when they arrived.
    - [ ] b.  There was a lot of snow everywhere.
    - [ ] c.  There was not much snow.
    - [ ] d.  There was no snow.

2.  Olivia thought her nose and fingers would freeze because
    - [ ] a.  she fell in the snow.
    - [ ] b.  she drank hot chocolate.
    - [ ] c.  she skied down the mountain.
    - [ ] d.  she didn't have a hat.

**WHAT CAN YOU DO?**  Color the stars.

I can draw conclusions to give me a deeper understanding of the text. ★★★

**KEY**
★  I need help.
★★  I can do this a little.
★★★  I can do this well.

# Get Ready to Write

## WRITING GOAL: Write an Opinion Essay

An opinion essay tells if you like or dislike something. Write your opinion in the introduction, your reasons in the body paragraphs, and a summary of your thoughts in the conclusion.

**A** Read the opinion essay. Underline words that connect two complete sentences.

**Writing Tip**
Use a comma and words like *and*, *but*, and *so* to connect two complete sentences.

**Introduction with opinion**

My favorite season is summer, and my favorite summer activity is going to the beach. There are so many fun activities to do at the beach.

**Body paragraphs with reasons**

When it's hot, I go swimming. I'm not very good at surfing the waves, but I love doing it. When it's cool, I like to have a picnic on the beach. I also like to build sandcastles. Sometimes I collect shells.

The only thing I don't like about the beach is the sun. Sometimes it's very strong, so I have to sit under an umbrella.

**Conclusion with summary**

On a cold day in the winter, when I have to stay in the house and drink hot chocolate, I dream about a hot, sunny day at the beach.

**B** Discuss the questions with a partner.

1. Why does the writer like going to the beach?
2. What is the writer's opinion about surfing the waves?
3. What activities do you enjoy doing most in summer?
4. Do you like summer or winter best? Why?

# Write

**C** Think about your favorite seasonal activity. Give your opinion about it. Fill in the chart.

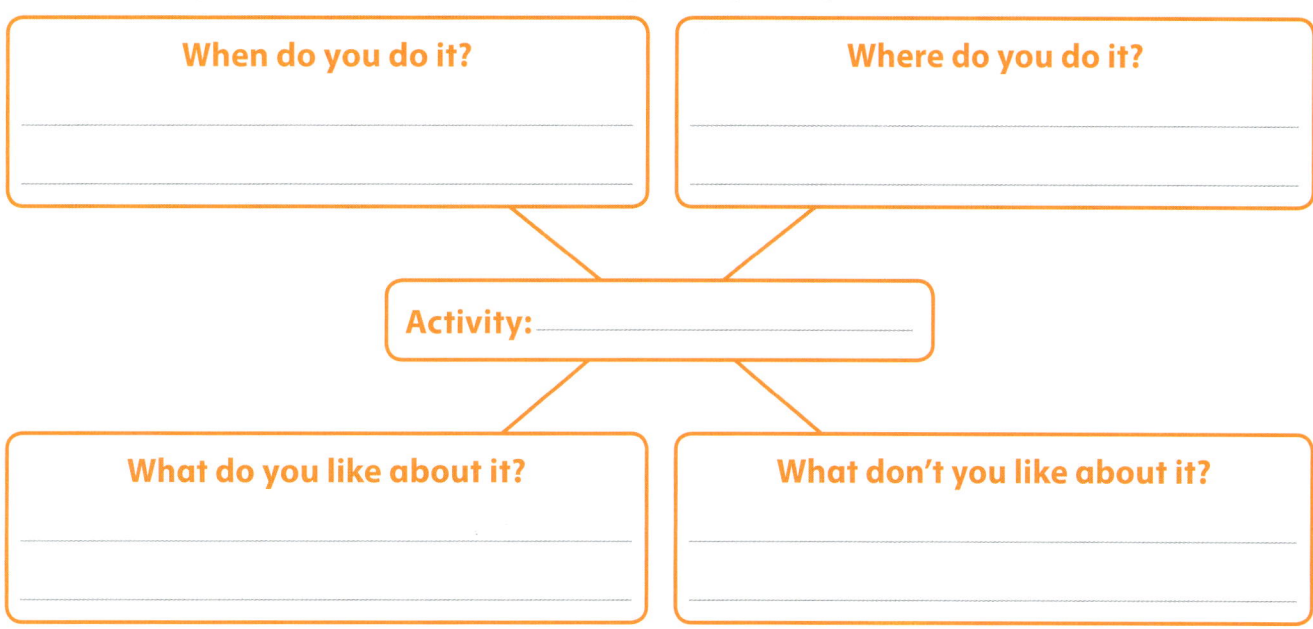

**When do you do it?**

_____

_____

**Where do you do it?**

_____

_____

**Activity:** _____

**What do you like about it?**

_____

_____

**What don't you like about it?**

_____

_____

**D** Write about your favorite seasonal activity. Use your words from **C**.
Choose new words, too.

1. What is your favorite seasonal activity?

   _____

2. When and where do you do it?

   _____

3. What do you like about it?

   _____

4. What don't you like about it?

   _____

Now write your opinion essay.

**WHAT CAN YOU DO?** Color the stars.

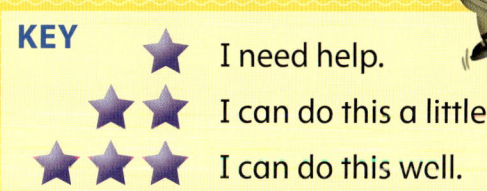

I can write an opinion essay about my
favorite seasonal activity. ⭐⭐⭐

I can use a comma and words like *and, but,*
and *so* to connect two sentences. ⭐⭐⭐

**KEY**

⭐ I need help.

⭐⭐ I can do this a little.

⭐⭐⭐ I can do this well.

TOPIC 5

MATH

# Our Five Senses

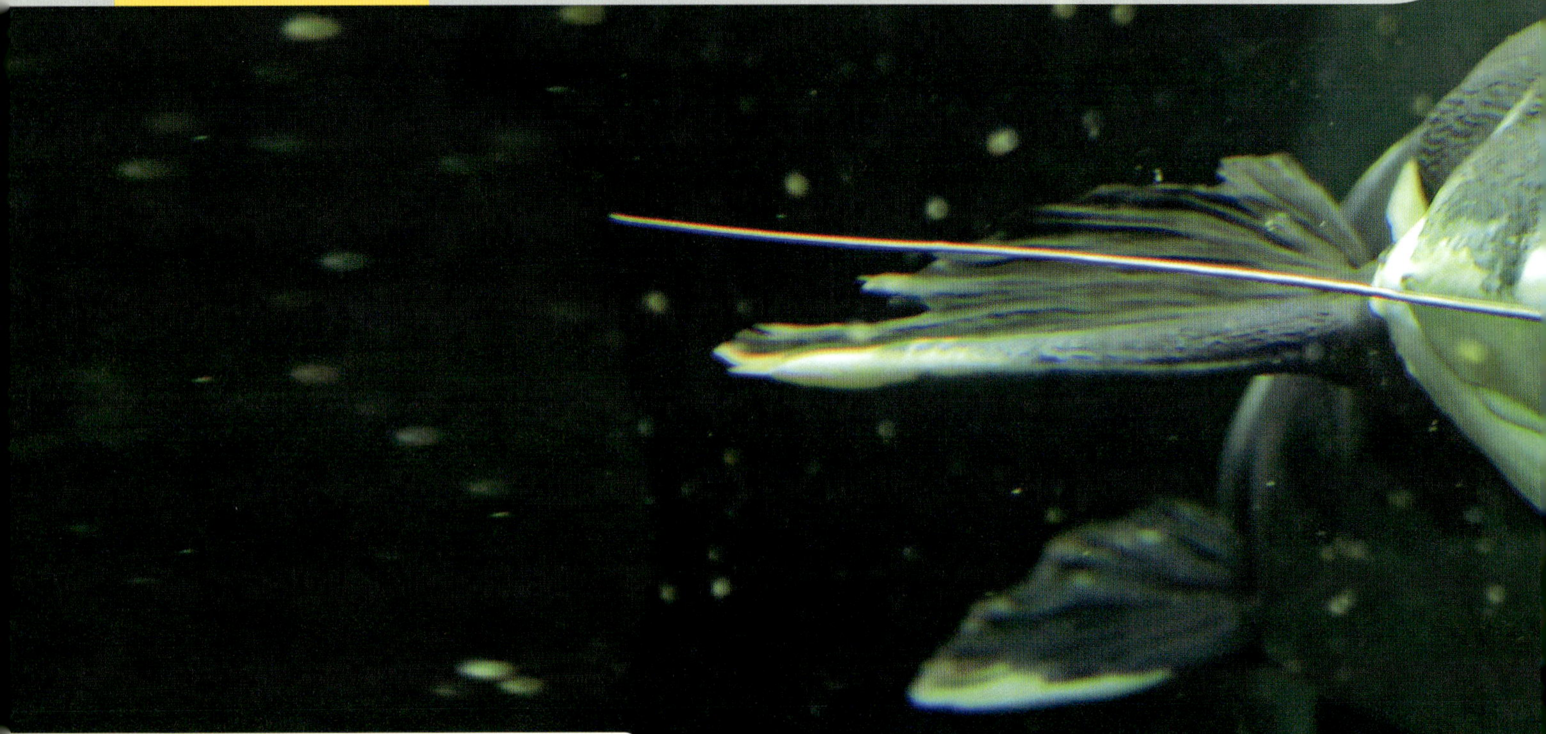

## MY GOALS

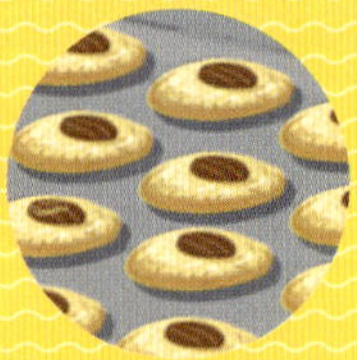

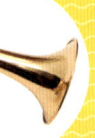

**UNIT 9**

- Read the story *Baking Cookies with Grandma*
- Scan for details

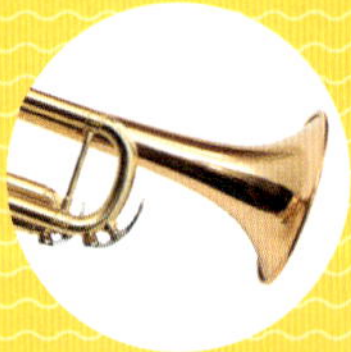

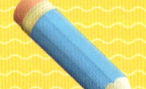

**UNIT 10**

- Read the article *Musical Instruments: Brass*
- Visualize

**WRITE**

- Write a descriptive essay

**A** Look at the picture.

1. What do you see? What's happening?
2. How is this fish similar to or different than other fish you have seen?

## A Taste of the River

Look at the catfish that lives at the bottom of a river. It has 20,000 taste buds on its tongue and 180,000 more on its body. Most are on the four pairs of whiskers around its mouth. Catfish use them to find and taste their food. To compare, humans have about 10,000 taste buds on their tongues that tell how things taste.

**B** Read the text.

1. How many taste buds does a catfish have compared to a human?

2. Where do catfish live?

3. What do catfish use their taste buds for?

**Think, Pair, Share**
What do you think it would be like to have taste buds all over your body?

# Read

## READING GOAL: Scan for Details

When you scan, you look quickly over the text for specific information. For example, if you need to find amounts, scan for numbers. After you read a text, scan the body paragraphs to find the information you need.

## Get Ready

**A** Read the paragraph below. Then scan for numbers. Choose the correct answer.

I went with three friends to the movies to see *The Galaxies*. The tickets cost $5.00 each. When we got to the movie theater, there were already more than 50 people in line.

1. How many friends did the writer go to the movies with?

   ☐ a. three
   ☐ b. four

2. How many people were in line when they got to the movie theater?

   ☐ a. less than 30
   ☐ b. more than 50

**B** Find the key words in the story. Look up the words you don't know in your dictionary.

**C** Read and listen to the story *Baking Cookies with Grandma*. 🔊 14

# Baking Cookies
## with Grandma

Grandma and Lin love to bake cookies. Today they are baking almond cookies. They make two dozen, or 24, cookies. They have 25 nuts. Lin puts one nut on
5   top of each cookie and eats the last one. Then they put the cookies in the oven and wait for them to be done.

"Something smells good," says Lin. "The cookies smell like butter. Are they done?"

10  "Almost," says Grandma. Five minutes later, she takes the cookies out of the oven. "They are golden brown. Let's taste them," Grandma says, as she takes one cookie and hands one cookie to Lin.

15  "They are soft and they taste sweet," says Lin. "And the nuts make them crunchy."

"Of course they're sweet," replies Grandma. "Almond cookies should never taste sour or spicy."

20     Lin finishes eating the cookie and exclaims, "Yum!" Then she opens the door to the yard and calls her brother, Billy, who is practicing outside with his soccer team.

     The soccer team, 11 boys and girls, enters the
25    kitchen quickly. Each child takes two cookies and says, "Thank you." Then they all go back outside. Lin looks sadly at the empty cookie pan. "The pan is empty!" she tells Grandma.

     "We'll just have to make more cookies!" exclaims
30    Grandma.

> **Scan** the text for the number that tells you who ate the cookies. Underline it.

**WHAT CAN YOU DO?**   Color the stars.

I can scan a text for specific information.
⭐⭐⭐

I can understand all the key words.
⭐⭐⭐

**KEY**

⭐   I need help.

⭐⭐   I can do this a little.

⭐⭐⭐   I can do this well.

# Understand

**Remember!**
When you need to find specific amounts, you can **scan** the text for numbers.

**A**  Think about scanning for details. Answer the questions and discuss with the class.

1. What numerals do you see in the first paragraph? What do they tell you?

2. How many children are on the soccer team?

3. How many cookies does the soccer team eat?

4. Why is scanning helpful?

**B**  Choose the correct answer.

1. What do Grandma and Lin love to do?
   - a. play soccer
   - b. bake cookies
   - c. eat nuts
   - d. buy groceries

2. How many nuts do they have?
   - a. 23
   - b. 24
   - c. 25
   - d. 26

3. What do the cookies smell like?
   - a. butter
   - b. almonds
   - c. sugar
   - d. cinnamon

4. How do the cookies taste?
   - a. spicy
   - b. sour
   - c. soft
   - d. sweet

**C**  Ask and answer the questions with a partner.

1. There are more nuts than cookies. How many more are there?

2. Why is the cookie pan empty after the boys and girls go back outside?

3. What's your favorite cookie?

4. Who in your family likes to bake? What do they bake?

**D** Complete the sentences.

> smells   taste   soft   sour   spicy   crunchy   sweet   smells like

Uncle Max has a bakery where everything (1) _____ delicious. My sister and
I visit the bakery on our way home from school. Today, the bakery (2) _____
chocolate because Uncle Max is baking chocolate cupcakes. When they come out of
the oven, he hands us each a hot, (3) _____ cupcake to (4) _____.
I like (5) _____ cupcakes with lots of sugar. My sister likes cupcakes with
(6) _____ nuts.

Once my uncle added chili peppers to the chocolate and the cupcakes were
(7) _____. So, I was wondering. If you add too much lemon, would the
cupcakes taste (8) _____?

**E** Read and complete the sentences with one, two,
or three words.

There is a tasting contest in town every year. The people in the
contest cover their eyes so they can't see. They taste ten items
and tell how each tastes and what it is. First, they taste strawberry pie. It tastes sweet.
Everyone knows it is strawberry pie. They each get five points. Next, they taste lemon candies.
Lemon candies taste sour. Many people know they are lemon candies. They get five more
points. The person who identifies the most items correctly wins. Today, one person names five
foods correctly, so she gets 25 points. The winner names eight foods, so he wins the contest
with 40 points.

1.  Scan the text for numbers. The winner names _____ foods correctly.

2.  The people in the contest cannot _____ the items.

3.  They tell how the items _____

4.  A strawberry pies tastes _____

5.  The person who names the _____ wins.

**WHAT CAN YOU DO?**  Color the stars.

I can scan a text after I read it to
find the information I need.
⭐⭐⭐

KEY

⭐  I need help.

⭐⭐  I can do this a little.

⭐⭐⭐  I can do this well.

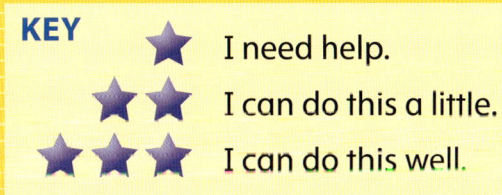

# Read

## READING GOAL: Visualize

Writers use words to help readers visualize, or create pictures in their minds. When you read, notice the words the writer uses to describe things. Try to see those things in your mind.

## Get Ready

**A** **Read the paragraph below. Choose the correct answer.**

Ana looked up and saw the sky full of clouds. She heard thunder and saw lightning. Suddenly, she felt a raindrop on her head.

1. What words help you visualize the sky?

   ☐ a. heard thunder

   ☐ b. full of clouds

2. What words help you visualize the storm?

   ☐ a. saw lightning

   ☐ b. looked up

**B** **Find the key words in the article. Look up the words you don't know in your dictionary.**

**C** **Read and listen to the article *Musical Instruments: Brass.* 🔊 15**

# Musical Instruments:

# Brass

All brass instruments are made of a metal called brass, so they look shiny. When you touch a brass instrument, it feels smooth. The brass musician blows into the instrument and the

5  air moves down a long tube to make a buzzing sound. The most popular brass instruments are the trumpet, the trombone, and the tuba.

## Trumpet

The trumpet has a long metal tube. The tube

10  bends around two times to form an oval shape that ends with a big opening. When you blow into a trumpet, the music sounds like buzzing. You can hear the wonderful sound of the trumpet when you listen to jazz music.

15 ## Trombone

The trombone feels like a trumpet, but it is bigger. It has a shiny, metal piece that slides in and out. The sound it makes changes as the musician moves the slide. You can hear

20  the pretty sounds of the trombone in bands, orchestras, and jazz groups.

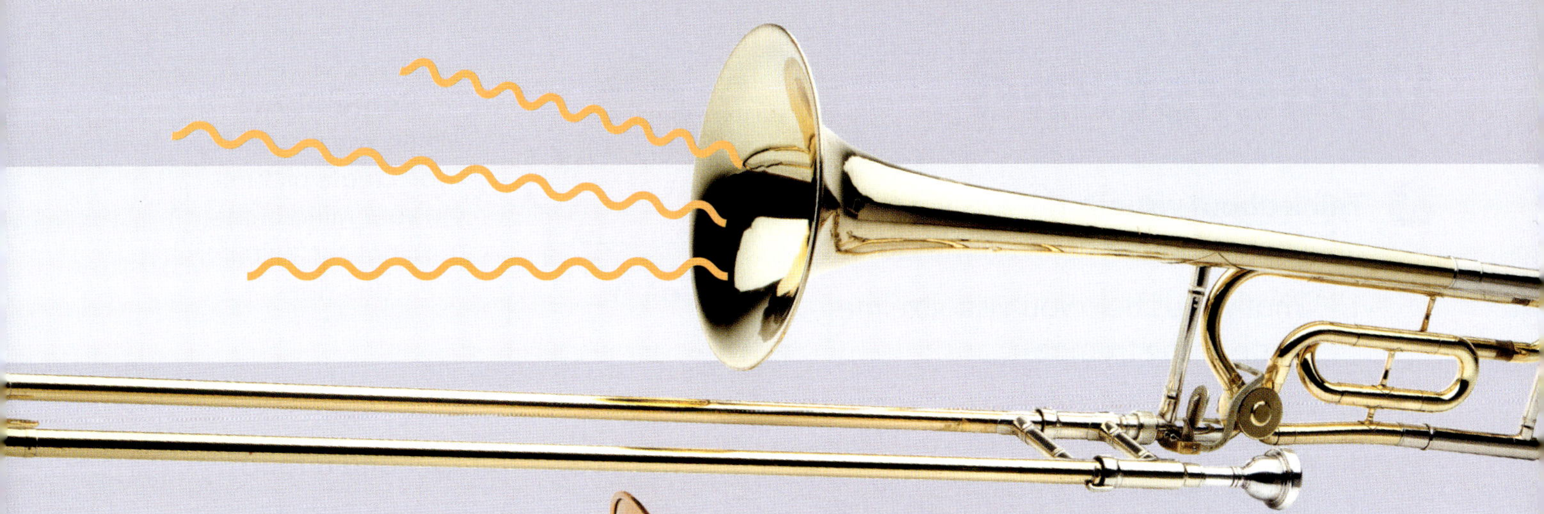

### Tuba

25 The tuba is the largest brass instrument. It looks similar to the trumpet with a tube that bends around. But both the tube and the opening are much bigger, and the sound it makes is much lower.

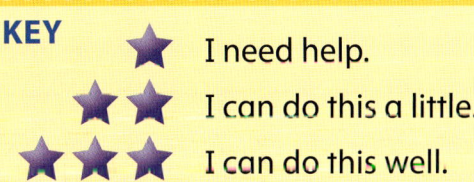

Can you create a picture in your mind of a musician playing a brass instrument? Describe it.

# Understand

**A**  **Think about visualizing. Answer the questions and discuss with the class.**

**Remember!**
When you **visualize**, you create pictures in your mind of the things the writer describes.

1. What words help you visualize the shape of the trumpet?

2. What words help you visualize the trombone?

3. What words help you visualize the difference between a trumpet and a tuba?

4. Why is it important to visualize when you read?

**B**  **Read. Choose T for True and F for False.**

1. Brass instruments are usually made of wood.                          T        F

2. A brass musician blows into the instrument to make music.            T        F

3. Brass instruments do not feel smooth.                                T        F

4. The trumpet has a big opening where the sound comes out.             T        F

5. Brass instruments make a buzzing sound.                              T        F

6. The trombone is smaller than the trumpet.                            T        F

7. The trombone has a metal piece that slides in and out.               T        F

8. A tuba is the largest brass instrument.                              T        F

**C**  **Ask and answer the questions with a partner.**

1. How are all brass instruments alike? How are they different?

2. How do people make sound with brass instruments?

3. What is the difference between a trumpet and a trombone?

4. What brass instrument would you like to play? Why?

**D** Choose the correct answer.

1. In line 2, *touch* means to
   - [ ] a. play an instrument.
   - [ ] b. listen to music.
   - [ ] c. put a hand on something.
   - [ ] d. smell with your nose.

2. In line 13, *hear* means to
   - [ ] a. receive sound through your ears.
   - [ ] b. see things with your eyes.
   - [ ] c. smell things with your nose.
   - [ ] d. touch things with your hand.

3. In line 13, *wonderful* means about the same as
   - [ ] a. extremely loud.
   - [ ] b. extremely long.
   - [ ] c. not very good.
   - [ ] d. extremely good.

4. In line 14, *listen* means to
   - [ ] a. try to see.
   - [ ] b. try to hear.
   - [ ] c. try to touch.
   - [ ] d. try to smell.

**E** Read the text. Then read the questions and choose the correct answer.

> Angela and I like playing guessing games. She covers my eyes so I can't see. Then she gives me an object, and I have to use my senses to tell what it is. First, I touch it. It's small. It has four legs, a head with short ears, and a long tail. It feels soft and furry, like a toy animal. Next, I shake it. *Meow! Meow!* It sounds like a kitten. I think it's a furry toy kitten. I open my eyes and look. I am correct. It is a white and orange toy kitten! Now it's Angela's turn to guess.

1. What words help you visualize the toy kitten?
   - [ ] a. small
   - [ ] b. soft and furry
   - [ ] c. four legs, a head with short ears, and a long tail
   - [ ] d. all of the above

2. What does the student do to identify the object?
   - [ ] a. looks at it
   - [ ] b. touches it and listens to it
   - [ ] c. listens to it and smells it
   - [ ] d. smells it and tastes it

**WHAT CAN YOU DO?** Color the stars.

I can notice the words the writer uses to describe things and visualize them. ★★★

KEY
★ I need help.
★★ I can do this a little.
★★★ I can do this well.

# Reading Check

**Remember!**
While you read, **visualize** to create pictures in your mind, and **scan for details** after you read to find specific information.

**A** Read and listen to the story. 🔊 16

## The Elmford–Winona Soccer Game

Look! The teams are on the field and the game is about to begin.

Listen! Did you hear the whistle? Elmford scores a goal in the first minute, so the score is 1–0. Winona gets the ball and scores. Elmford's goalie doesn't even touch the ball and it's an easy goal for Winona. The score is tied, 1–1.

It is halftime and the score is 2–1 with Elmford leading. I love the smell of stadium hot dogs. I can't wait to enjoy a sweet and spicy one. They taste amazing!

We're back. The second half is exciting. With just 45 seconds left in the game, the score is Elmford 3, Winona 1.

And there's the whistle! Elmford wins the game 3–1!

**B** Read the text again. Then choose the correct answer.

1. Read the first sentence again. What does the writer want you to do?

   ☐ a. visualize      ☐ b. scan for a detail

2. How do you find the final score of the game after reading the text?

   ☐ a. visualize      ☐ b. scan for details

**C** Answer the questions and discuss your answers with the class.

1. Who wins the game and by how many points do they win?

2. Describe what the players are doing when Winona scores a goal.

**D** Choose the correct answer.

1. When did Elmford score the first goal?
   - ☐ a. in the first minute of the game
   - ☐ b. right before halftime
   - ☐ c. right after halftime
   - ☐ d. in the last minute of the game

2. Elmford's goalie
   - ☐ a. dropped the ball.
   - ☐ b. kicked the ball.
   - ☐ c. didn't see the ball.
   - ☐ d. didn't touch the ball.

3. What was the score at halftime?
   - ☐ a. Elmford 1, Winona 1
   - ☐ b. Elmford 1, Winona 2
   - ☐ c. Elmford 2, Winona 1
   - ☐ d. Elmford 3, Winona 1

4. What do stadium hotdogs taste like?
   - ☐ a. They taste sour.
   - ☐ b. They taste crunchy.
   - ☐ c. They taste sweet and spicy.
   - ☐ d. They taste like burgers.

**E** Discuss with a partner.

1. Which team plays better? How do you know?

2. What does the person telling about the soccer game think about stadium hotdogs? How do you know?

**F** Choose the best word.

My Auntie Anika has a small restaurant in town. I like to
(1. **listen** / **hear**) to her working in the kitchen. Her bracelets
clink as she chops and cooks the food. She makes lots of (2. **soft** /
**wonderful**) dishes. She uses chili peppers to make (3. **spicy** / **sweet**) dishes.
She uses lemons to make (4. **crunchy** / **sour**) dishes and sugar to make (5. **sweet** /
**sour**) desserts. The tables in the restaurant are set with tablecloths and candles. They
look very (6. **spicy** / **pretty**). And all of the dishes (7. **taste** / **feel**) delicious!

---

**WHAT CAN YOU DO?** Color the stars.

I can scan for details. ⭐⭐⭐

I can visualize. ⭐⭐⭐

**KEY**

 I need help.

 I can do this a little.

 I can do this well.

# Get Ready to Write

## WRITING GOAL: Write a Descriptive Essay

A descriptive essay describes a person, place, or thing. Use describing words and details to paint a picture in your reader's mind. Describing words help your writing to be interesting.

**A**  Read the descriptive essay. Underline the words that show what the writer can see, hear, touch, smell, and taste.

**Writing Tip**
Use your senses (what you see, hear, touch, smell, or taste) to describe your topic.

Introduction of the essay topic

Sunset Beach is the most wonderful place I know. When you visit this beach, it takes your mind off everything and you can relax.

Body with describing words and details

The sun shines in the blue sky and lights up the deep, blue-green water. If you look closely, you can see pretty little shells on the warm, white sand.

As I walk along the beach, I hear the waves breaking on the shore and children laughing as they play in the water. I feel the warm ocean breezes. I love the way the sand feels as it slides between my toes, so soft and warm.

The ocean water smells salty. Sometimes I can smell fish grilling in the beach restaurants. I like to taste different kinds of fish. But more than anything, I love to swim in the ocean.

Conclusion with final thought

I can't think of anything I enjoy more than a day at Sunset Beach!

**B**  Discuss the questions with a partner.

1. What does the writer see at the beach?

2. What does the writer hear at the beach?

3. What other senses does the writer use at the beach?

4. What is the writer's favorite thing to do at the beach?

# Write

**C** Think about your favorite place. Use your five senses to describe it. Fill in the chart.

| see | hear | feel | smell | taste |
|---|---|---|---|---|
| | | | | |
| | | | | |
| | | | | |
| | | | | |

**D** Write about your favorite place. Use your words from **C**. Choose new words, too.

1. What does your favorite place look like?

   _____

2. What sounds do you hear there?

   _____

3. Are there special smells or tastes at your favorite place?

   _____

4. What do you like best about it?

   _____

Now write your descriptive essay.

**WHAT CAN YOU DO?** Color the stars.

I can write a descriptive essay.
★★★

I can use my senses to describe my favorite place. ★★★

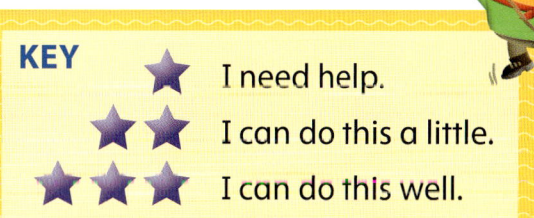

KEY
★ I need help.
★★ I can do this a little.
★★★ I can do this well.

# See the World!

## MY GOALS

### UNIT 11

- Read the essay *Our Trip to Egypt*
- Take notes

### UNIT 12

- Read the story *Adventure in Oaxaca*
- Identify characters, setting, and plot

### WRITE

- Write a story

**A** Look at the picture.

1. What do you see?

2. Can you guess what any of the hieroglyphics mean?

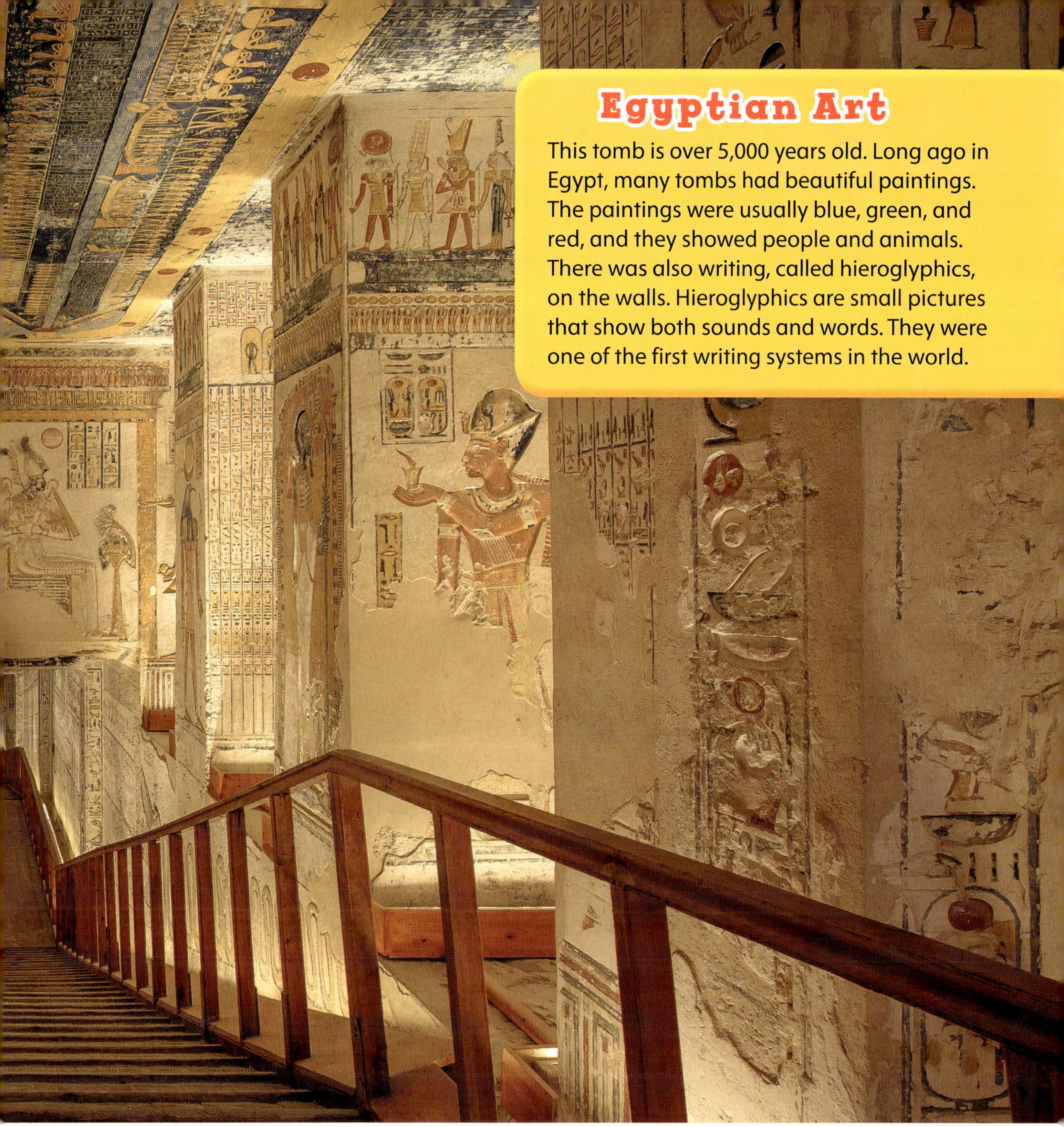

## Egyptian Art

This tomb is over 5,000 years old. Long ago in Egypt, many tombs had beautiful paintings. The paintings were usually blue, green, and red, and they showed people and animals. There was also writing, called hieroglyphics, on the walls. Hieroglyphics are small pictures that show both sounds and words. They were one of the first writing systems in the world.

**B**  **Read the text.**

1. How old is the tomb?

2. What did the tombs have on the walls?

3. What did you learn about hieroglyphics?

**Think, Pair, Share**
Would you like to write with hieroglyphics? Why or why not?

# Read

## READING GOAL: Take Notes

Taking notes will help you remember important information. When you read, underline important details. Then, to take notes, write a few words about these details on a separate piece of paper.

## Get Ready

**A**  **Read the paragraph below. Choose the correct answer.**

The Incas lived in Peru between AD 1400 and 1533. They built a city called Machu Picchu on top of a mountain.

1.  *Incas are from Peru. They built Machu Picchu.* Are these notes good or bad?

    ☐  a.  good notes

    ☐  b.  bad notes

2.  *A city on a mountain. 1400 and 1533.* Are these notes good or bad?

    ☐  a.  good notes

    ☐  b.  bad notes

**B**  **Find the key words in the essay. Look up the words you don't know in your dictionary.**

**C**  **Read and listen to the essay *Our Trip to Egypt*. 🔊 17**

# Our Trip to Egypt

In the spring, my family began to plan our summer vacation. Mom wanted to visit Hawaii. She wanted to surf the waves. Dad wanted to visit China. He wanted to see the
5   Great Wall, and he loves Chinese dishes with tofu even though he cannot pick up the tofu with his chopsticks. My sister, Mia, and I preferred to visit Egypt. Finally, we all agreed to go to Egypt. We planned our trip and went
10  in June.

We flew to Cairo in northern Egypt. The weather was hot and humid. We spent a few days in Cairo exploring the city. We bought kebabs from street vendors. Kebabs are made
15  with meat and spices, and they are grilled. They were delicious!

One day, we went to Giza to see the pyramids. They are the largest pyramids in Egypt. They were built about 5,000 years
20  ago. Over 100,000 people worked to build them. They are amazing!

What are some important details about the trip? Underline them. Then write some **notes** on a separate piece of paper.

Mia and I wanted to <mark>ride a camel</mark>. Finally, my parents decided we could all ride camels across the sand and around the pyramids. The camel ride was bumpy, but it was exciting.

25

We saw lots of amazing sights and ate delicious foods in Egypt. It was my favorite trip ever.

## WHAT CAN YOU DO?   Color the stars.

I can take notes.

I can understand all the key words.

KEY

 I need help.

 I can do this a little.

★★★ I can do this well.

# Understand

**Remember!**
When you read, underline important details. Then write a few words about them on a separate piece of paper.

**A**  Look at your notes for *Our Trip to Egypt.* Answer the questions and discuss with the class.

1. What did you underline in the first two paragraphs?

2. What notes did you write?

3. What notes did you write about what the family did in Egypt?

4. Why is it helpful to take notes as you read?

**B**  Choose the correct answer.

1. When did the family go to Egypt?

   ☐ a. in the fall
   ☐ b. in the winter
   ☐ c. in the spring
   ☐ d. in the summer

2. What food did they buy from street vendors in Cairo?

   ☐ a. kebabs
   ☐ b. burgers
   ☐ c. sushi
   ☐ d. spaghetti

3. When were the pyramids in Giza built?

   ☐ a. about 50 years ago
   ☐ b. about 500 years ago
   ☐ c. about 5,000 years ago
   ☐ d. about 10,000 years ago

4. How was the camel ride?

   ☐ a. bumpy but exciting
   ☐ b. fun
   ☐ c. scary
   ☐ d. boring

**C**  Ask and answer the questions with a partner.

1. Why did different family members want to go to different places?

2. What new things did the family see and do in Egypt?

3. Why are the pyramids in Giza amazing?

**D** Complete the sentences.

China   Egypt   tofu   Hawaii   camel   pyramids   chopsticks   vendors

I love to play Around the World with my friend Amy. In the game, the first place we visit is Giza, in (1) _____. We go there to see the (2) _____, the largest ones in Egypt. Another exciting thing you can do there is ride a (3) _____. It's bumpy but fun.

Next we go to Asia and visit (4) _____. It is a very large country where people use (5) _____ to eat. One very popular food is (6) _____, which looks like a small, white block. Street (7) _____ sell cold rice noodles and grilled meat.

The last place we visit in Around the World is (8) _____, a group of islands in the Pacific Ocean. They are part of the United States, and people go there to see the volcanoes and surf in the waves.

**E** Read and complete the sentences with one, two, or three words.

Alex:   I'm going to China this summer on a homestay.
Liam:   Have you been there before?
Alex:   No, it's my first time. I'm very excited about the trip. But, I don't speak Chinese!
Liam:   That's okay! You'll learn. You'll have to try new foods, too. Have you ever eaten tofu or rice cakes?
Alex:   No, I haven't. I will learn so much about Chinese customs this summer.

1. This conversation is about a _____

2. Alex is very _____ about the trip.

3. Alex does not speak _____

4. He has never eaten tofu or _____

**WHAT CAN YOU DO?**   Color the stars.

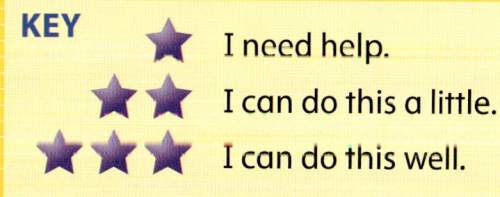

I can take notes about important details to help me remember things better. ★★★

**KEY**   ★ I need help.
★★ I can do this a little.
★★★ I can do this well.

# Read

## READING GOAL: Identify Characters, Setting, and Plot

The characters are the people in the story. The setting is where and when the story happens. The plot is what happens in the story. Identify characters, setting, and plot to understand a story more.

## Get Ready

**A** Choose the correct answer.

1. An example of a character is
   - ☐ a. Bao, a student on a homestay in Canada.
   - ☐ b. visiting a science museum.

2. An example of a setting is
   - ☐ a. Andy and his cousin Hugo.
   - ☐ b. Italy in the spring.

3. An example of a plot is
   - ☐ a. a man travels to Thailand and sees elephants.
   - ☐ b. the jungles of Thailand.

**B** Find the key words in the story. Look up the words you don't know in your dictionary.

**C** Read and listen to the story *Adventure in Oaxaca*. 🔊 18

## Adventure in Oaxaca

Adele's dad is from Mexico. Every spring, Adele's family goes to Mexico to visit family. They stay with her grandparents in Oaxaca.

Oaxaca is a beautiful old city. This year, Adele
5 and her brother, Andres, are old enough to go exploring without their parents.

"You can walk around town," says Mom. "But first, let's have lunch. Grandpa Juan is making tacos."

10 Tacos are thin pancakes made from corn that have meat, chicken, or vegetables inside. They are like crepes, but crepes are from France. Adele's mom loves crepes, too. She makes them with cheese or eggs.

15 After lunch, Adele and Andres explore the town. They walk for hours and see amazing things.

"I'm tired. Let's go home," says Adele. "Do you know the way?"

"We are here," says Andres, pointing to the map,
20 "but I don't see Grandma's street."

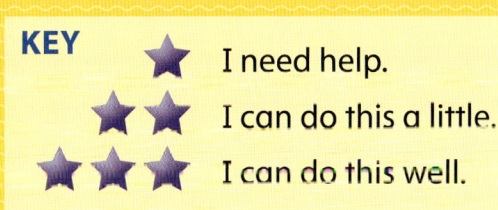

"Oh, no! We're lost!" cries Adele. "What will we do?"

Adele thinks. "I know," she says. "When my friend Ani was lost in India, she asked a man with a rickshaw, a kind of bicycle with three wheels, for help. He drove her home."

"Let's ask the taxi driver," says Andres.

The taxi driver drives the children to Grandma's house. They had a wonderful adventure.

25

> Who are the two **main characters** in this story? What other characters are there?

## WHAT CAN YOU DO?  Color the stars.

I can understand the story. ★★★

I can understand all the key words. ★★★

**KEY**

★ I need help.

★★ I can do this a little.

★★★ I can do this well.

# Understand

**A** Think about identifying the characters, setting, and plot. Answer the questions and discuss with the class.

1. Where and when does the story happen?
2. What is the problem in this story?
3. How do Adele and Andres resolve their problem?
4. Why is it important to identify the characters, setting, and plot in a story?

**B** Read. Choose T for True and F for False.

| | | |
|---|---|---|
| 1. Adele's dad is from India. | T | F |
| 2. Adele's mom loves crepes. | T | F |
| 3. Every year, Adele's family goes to Mexico to visit family. | T | F |
| 4. Tacos and crepes are similar. | T | F |
| 5. The whole family explores the town together. | T | F |
| 6. There are beautiful buildings and squares in Oaxaca. | T | F |
| 7. Adele and Andres don't have a map. | T | F |
| 8. They can't find Grandma's street on the map. | T | F |

**C** Ask and answer the questions with a partner.

1. Why is this family visit to Oaxaca different from other years?
2. How do you find the way home on a map?
3. What does Adele learn from her friend Ani?
4. How are tacos and crepes alike? How are they different?

**D** Choose the correct answer.

1. In line 4, the word that means about the same as *very pretty* is

   - ☐ a. old.
   - ☐ b. beautiful.
   - ☐ c. city.
   - ☐ d. brother.

2. In line 9, *tacos* are from

   - ☐ a. France.
   - ☐ b. India.
   - ☐ c. Mexico.
   - ☐ d. Japan.

3. In line 12, what are *crepes*?

   - ☐ a. very thin pancakes with cheese or eggs inside
   - ☐ b. thin pancakes made from corn
   - ☐ c. a dish made with noodles
   - ☐ d. a spicy meat dish popular in India

4. In line 24, a *rickshaw* is

   - ☐ a. a boat in China.
   - ☐ b. a truck in Mexico.
   - ☐ c. a fast train in France.
   - ☐ d. a kind of bicycle with three wheels in India.

**E** Read the text. Then read the questions and choose the correct answer.

Dear Adele,

Last week, we went to visit my grandmother in Kerala, India. She took us on a houseboat tour on the river. We saw many villages and fishermen. When we were very far from home, we ran out of gas! I was worried we wouldn't make it back. But my cousin's friend brought us more gas. I was so happy! See you soon!

Ani

1. Where does the story happen?

   - ☐ a. in Kerala, India
   - ☐ b. in a village
   - ☐ c. in pictures
   - ☐ d. in Ani's grandmother's home

2. Why was Ani worried?

   - ☐ a. The village was far away.
   - ☐ b. The houseboat was too big.
   - ☐ c. They ran out of gas.
   - ☐ d. Her cousins got lost.

## WHAT CAN YOU DO? Color the stars.

I can identify characters, setting, and plot to understand a story more. ⭐⭐⭐

KEY
⭐ I need help.
⭐⭐ I can do this a little.
⭐⭐⭐ I can do this well.

# Reading Check

**A** Read and listen to the story.  19

## A Day in Paris, France

Kathy works at Sunshine Travel in Toronto, Canada. Many people who visit Sunshine Travel want to go see the pyramids and ride a camel in Egypt. So Kathy takes a group there. She buys airplane tickets to Egypt with a two-hour stop in Paris, France.

On Wednesday, the people who work in the airport in Paris tell Kathy that there are sandstorms in Egypt.

"We'll have to stay in Paris until the storms are over," Kathy tells the group. "We'll have fun. Tonight we'll eat crepes for dinner, and tomorrow we'll visit the Eiffel Tower."

Kathy takes the group to the hotel for dinner. The next day they see beautiful places. Everyone has a great time.

"The storms are over," Kathy tells them on Thursday night. "In the morning we leave for Egypt."

**B** Read the text again. Then choose the correct answer.

1. You underline and write down the words *Egypt* and *France*. What are you doing?

   ☐ a. taking notes      ☐ b. identifying characters, setting, and plot

2. You think about how Kathy shows the group Paris when they can't go on to Egypt. What are you doing?

   ☐ a. taking notes      ☐ b. identifying characters, setting, and plot

**C** Answer the questions and discuss your answers with the class.

1. What would you underline and what notes would you write down to help you remember the story better?

2. What is the plot of this story?

**D** Choose the correct answer.

1. Where does Kathy work?
   - ☐ a. at a movie theater
   - ☐ b. on an airplane
   - ☐ c. at a travel agency
   - ☐ d. at an amusement park

2. Where do people who visit Sunshine Travel want to go?
   - ☐ a. Egypt
   - ☐ b. Canada
   - ☐ c. France
   - ☐ d. India

3. Why does the group have to stay in Paris?
   - ☐ a. because they want to eat crepes
   - ☐ b. because there is a blizzard in Egypt
   - ☐ c. because the airplane was broken
   - ☐ d. because there are sandstorms in Egypt

4. What do they eat for dinner in Paris?
   - ☐ a. tacos
   - ☐ b. crepes
   - ☐ c. curry
   - ☐ d. sushi

**E** Discuss with a partner.

1. What problem does the main character solve?

2. What is the main setting in the story?

3. Would you like to go to Paris or Egypt? Why?

**F** Choose the best word.

You can see pyramids in Mexico and (1. **Egypt / France**) and eat (2. **tacos / crepes**) in France. People in (3. **China / Hawaii**) and Japan eat their food with (4. **forks / chopsticks**). In Egypt you can (5. **ride a camel / ride in a rickshaw**) and eat kebabs made by (6. **street vendors / rickshaw drivers**). Everywhere you go, you can see and taste exciting new things!

**WHAT CAN YOU DO?** Color the stars.

I can take notes.
★★★

I can identify characters, setting, and plot.
★★★

KEY
★ I need help.
★★ I can do this a little.
★★★ I can do this well.

# Get Ready to Write

**WRITING GOAL: Write a Story**

A story can be about real or imaginary characters. Usually the characters in a story need to solve a problem. The problem can be caused by the setting or the plot.

**A** Read the story. Underline pronouns like *he*, *she*, and *they*.

> **Writing Tip**
> Use pronouns like *he*, *she*, and *they* to avoid repeating names.

**Character in the story**

Last spring <u>Emily</u> went to India to visit family. Emily loved her aunt and uncle, and she liked playing with her cousin Nabil.

One morning, Nabil took Emily into town. They saw beautiful parks and ate food from a street vendor. After lunch, Emily wanted to ride a camel, but Nabil said it wasn't safe. So they climbed into a rickshaw.

**Problem in the story**

**How the problem was solved**

The driver drove very fast. Suddenly, <u>a man stepped into the street, but he didn't see the rickshaw</u>. Emily closed her eyes. She was afraid the rickshaw was going to hit him. The rickshaw got closer and closer and, at the last second, <u>the driver turned left</u>.

When Emily opened her eyes, they were in front of Nabil's house. Camels may not be safe, but rickshaws are scary!

**B** Discuss the questions with a partner.

1. What did Emily and Nabil do in town?
2. Why did they decide to take a rickshaw?
3. What was the problem with the rickshaw?
4. How did Emily feel when they got home?

# Write

**C** Think about a travel experience you can tell a story about. Complete the chart.

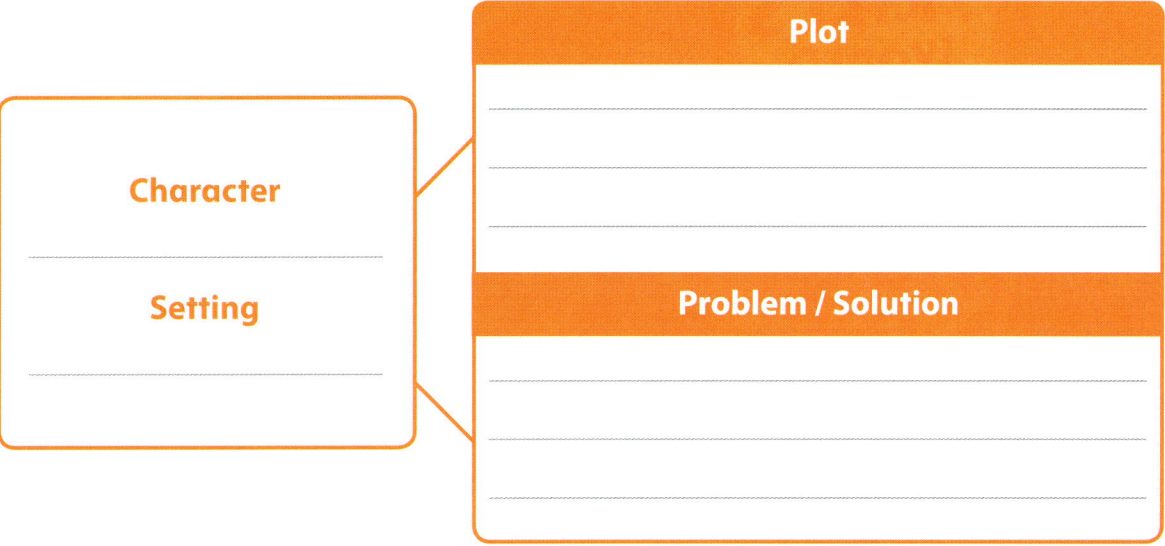

**D** Write a story about your travel experience. Use your words from **C**. Choose new words, too. Tell what happens to the characters in the story.

1. Who is the character?

   _____

2. When and where does the experience happen?

   _____

3. What problem does the character have?

   _____

4. How is the problem resolved?

   _____

**Now write your story.**

**WHAT CAN YOU DO?** Color the stars.

I can write a story. ★★★

I can use pronouns like *he*, *she*, and *they* to avoid repeating names. ★★★

**KEY**
★ I need help.
★★ I can do this a little.
★★★ I can do this well.

# Reading 5
## with Writing

# Workbook

## Elise Pritchard

OXFORD
UNIVERSITY PRESS

# Read

**READING GOAL:**
**Paraphrase**

**Remember!**
**Paraphrasing** is putting something into your own words.

**A** Read the article. Then retell the information in your own words.

## Snacks: Good or Bad?

Who doesn't enjoy eating a snack between meals? An apple, some carrots, a glass of milk, or a piece of cheese are all healthy snacks. Snack time is a favorite time of the day for many people! Children who are very active can eat one or more snacks during the day. This helps them keep up their energy levels so they can do exercise and play sports. But some people say it's not good to eat between meals. They think that children who eat too many snacks will not be hungry for dinner. So it's important to remember to eat enough snacks that you have lots of energy, but not so many that you cannot eat your dinner.

**B** Choose the correct answer.

1. This article talks about whether eating snacks between meals is good or bad.
   ☑ a. true     ☐ b. false     ☐ c. doesn't say

2. A lot of people enjoy eating snacks.
   ☐ a. true     ☐ b. false     ☐ c. doesn't say

3. Active children should eat at least four snacks a day.
   ☐ a. true     ☐ b. false     ☐ c. doesn't say

4. Eating snacks can make you sleepy.
   ☐ a. true     ☐ b. false     ☐ c. doesn't say

5. Children who eat too many snacks may not be hungry for dinner.
   ☐ a. true     ☐ b. false     ☐ c. doesn't say

6. Eating a little food often may be healthier than eating three full meals a day.
   ☐ a. true     ☐ b. false     ☐ c. doesn't say

**C** Answer the questions. Use full sentences.

1.  What are some healthy snacks?

    An apple, carrots, a glass of milk, and a piece of cheese are healthy snacks.

2.  How does eating a snack help you?

    _____

3.  Why is it important to keep up your energy level?

    _____

4.  Why do some people think eating snacks isn't good for you?

    _____

5.  What does the writer think about eating snacks?

    _____

**D** Read the text. Choose the correct words to fill each blank.

### A Trip to the Mall

Saturday morning, I went to the mall with my mom. We wanted to buy presents for Aunt Mae and Uncle Todd. We bought a book about asteroids for Uncle Todd and then stopped for lunch. I had (1) _____ with mushrooms. Mom had an apple and (2) _____ to eat and (3) _____ with milk and sugar to drink.

Later I wanted (4) _____ for a snack, but mom said they weren't healthy. In the end, we bought a box of chocolates for Aunt Mae and a banana for me.

1.  ☑ a. a piece of pizza
    ☐ b. a piece of cheese
    ☐ c. a box of chocolates

2.  ☐ a. a glass of milk
    ☐ b. a bottle of water
    ☐ c. a piece of cheese

3.  ☐ a. a bag of potato chips
    ☐ b. a cup of coffee
    ☐ c. a piece of pizza

4.  ☐ a. a bottle of water
    ☐ b. a glass of milk
    ☐ c. a bag of potato chips

**E** Unscramble and match.

1.  n e b a •                          • a. a healthy food

    _____

2.  a l g s a s f o k i l m •          • b. a healthy drink

    _____

# Read

**READING GOAL:
Use the 5 Ws**

**A** Read. Notice the 5 Ws while you read.

# Up, Up, and Away!

## Please come to my birthday party

You are invited to fly with me to the moon to celebrate my birthday! Friends and space explorers should meet at my house. We will climb into a rocket in my backyard and take off for a flight to the moon. My mom made snacks for us to eat during the trip. There will be cupcakes, cheese, nuts, and bags of pretzels. Please come dressed as an astronaut or other space traveler. I hope you can all join me on my flight to the moon.

| | |
|---|---|
| **When:** | June 5 at 5:00 p.m. |
| **Where:** | 324 Walnut Street |
| **What:** | A flight to the moon |
| **From:** | Julia |
| **To:** | Friends and space explorers |

**B** Choose the correct answer.

1. When is Julia's party?
   - ☐ a. June 4 at 5:00 p.m.
   - ☑ b. June 5 at 5:00 p.m.
   - ☐ c. June 5 at 7:00 p.m.

2. Where is Julia's party?
   - ☐ a. at 324 Walnut Street
   - ☐ b. at school
   - ☐ c. at the library

3. Who is invited to the party?
   - ☐ a. Julia's grandparents
   - ☐ b. Julia's friends
   - ☐ c. Julia's brother and sister

4. What are they going to do?
   - ☐ a. play party games
   - ☐ b. go swimming
   - ☐ c. climb into a rocket and fly to the moon

**C** Complete the sentences with one, two, or three words.

1. Julia had a party to celebrate _____her birthday._____

2. Julia sent party _____ to her friends.

3. The children met at _____

4. The rocket was in Julia's _____

5. Her mom made _____ for them to eat during the trip.

6. There were cupcakes, cheese, nuts, and _____

**D** Choose the words that complete the sentences.

| ~~noodles~~   bottles of soda |

1. _____Noodles_____ are long, thin pieces of food cooked in hot water.

2. When we are thirsty, we like to drink _____

| bags of pretzels   nuts |

3. Peanuts and walnuts are types of _____

4. _____ are full of salty snacks that can be shaped like sticks.

**E** Read the clues. Write the word.

1. These are small round food that you can eat with noodles.

   _____meatballs_____

2. This is a small round dessert that you can eat at parties.

   _____

3. A food from Japan that has fish and rice.

   _____

# Write

Circle the transitions.

1. I love apples. In fact, apples are my favorite fruit.

2. Cupcakes are delicious. Nuts are good, as well.

3. Noodles are eaten in Korea. They are also popular in China.

> **Remember!**
> Use transitions like *also*, *in fact*, and *as well* to introduce more information.

# Read

**READING GOAL:**
**Make Connections**

**A** Read the movie review. Make connections with your own experiences.

## The Future of Polar Bears

*Polar Bears in Danger* is a very informative movie. It tells all about polar bears: where they live, what they eat, and how they survive in such cold climates. Polar bears are the largest kind of bear and they are the best swimmers. These mammals live in the icy Arctic, on the sea ice. It is very beautiful. The photography in the movie is amazing. There is bright white snow as far as you can see.

The movie shows how the sea ice is melting. It explains that, as the areas of sea ice get smaller and smaller, there are fewer places for the polar bears to live. With less ice, it is getting harder and harder for the polar bears to stay alive.

**B** Choose the correct answer.

1. Polar bears, like humans, are mammals. Both have hair or fur, and they breathe air.

   ☐ a. true     ☐ b. false     ☐ c. doesn't say

2. Polar bears are not very good swimmers.

   ☐ a. true     ☐ b. false     ☐ c. doesn't say

3. Polar bears eat seal fat.

   ☐ a. true     ☐ b. false     ☐ c. doesn't say

4. The movie has poor photography.

   ☐ a. true     ☐ b. false     ☐ c. doesn't say

5. The movie shows pictures of the sea ice melting.

   ☐ a. true     ☐ b. false     ☐ c. doesn't say

6. The writer thinks the movie is very informative.

   ☐ a. true     ☐ b. false     ☐ c. doesn't say

**C** Answer the questions. Use full sentences.

1. What is the name of the movie?

   _____

2. What is the movie about?

   _____

3. What is the polar bears' environment like?

   _____

4. What is happening to the polar bears' environment?

   _____

5. What will happen to the polar bears if the sea ice melts?

   _____

**D** Read the text. Choose the correct word to fill each blank.

### The Life Cycle of a Butterfly

A (1) _____ is a beautiful insect. But where does it come from? Adult butterflies lay eggs on the leaves of plants. When the egg hatches, a (2) _____ comes out. Caterpillars eat a lot of leaves and get (3) _____, up to 100 times their size when they came out of the egg. When it is fully grown, the caterpillar forms a chrysalis. The shell around the chrysalis hardens to protect it from predators, like (4) _____. Finally, the chrysalis splits open and a butterfly flies out.

1. ☐ a. butterfly
   ☐ b. lizard
   ☐ c. squirrel

2. ☐ a. polar bear
   ☐ b. squirrel
   ☐ c. caterpillar

3. ☐ a. faster
   ☐ b. larger
   ☐ c. smaller

4. ☐ a. jaguars
   ☐ b. lizards
   ☐ c. polar bears

**E** Unscramble and match.

1. j g a r u a •

   _____

2. q s u r i r l e •

   _____

• a. an animal that is the same color as a tree branch

• b. an animal that lives in the forest and has spots

# Read

**READING GOAL:**
**Classify and Categorize**

**Remember!**
**Classifying and categorizing** things into groups will help you understand how they are similar and different.

**A** Read. Classify and categorize things that are alike while you read.

## A Day at the Zoo

Our class went on a trip to the zoo. We saw lots of environments and some amazing animals.

First, we visited the African animal area. We saw giraffes, zebras, lions, gazelles, and cheetahs. Our guide told us that the cheetah is the fastest animal in the world.

Then we visited the monkey house. We saw monkeys, gorillas, and orangutans. The monkeys were the funniest animals. They made funny faces, and they swung from tree to tree.

Next we went to the reptile house. We saw crocodiles, lizards, and snakes. The largest crocodile lives in the sea. It can weigh about 1,800 kg. We saw a smaller crocodile and a giant tortoise, too.

We were tired but happy after our day at the zoo.

**B** Choose the correct answer.

1. How were the giraffes, zebras, lions, gazelles, and cheetahs alike?

☐ a. They were all in the African animal area.

☐ b. They were all in the monkey house.

☐ c. They were all in the reptile house.

2. What is the fastest animal in the world?

☐ a. a cheetah

☐ b. a giraffe

☐ c. a zebra

3. Why did the students think the monkeys were funny?

☐ a. They ate bananas.

☐ b. They made funny sounds.

☐ c. They made funny faces.

4. What animals did the students see in the reptile house?

☐ a. crocodiles and lizards

☐ b. snakes and a giant tortoise

☐ c. both of the above

**C** Complete the sentences with one, two, or three words.

1. The class went on a trip _____

2. They thought the animals were _____

3. They saw monkeys, gorillas, and orangutans in the _____

4. They saw _____ swinging from trees.

5. In the reptile house, they saw a small crocodile and a giant _____

6. They were _____ after a day at the zoo.

**D** Choose a word and complete the sentences.

| faster    fastest |

1. A gazelle runs _____ than a camel.

2. A cheetah is the _____ animal in the world.

| dolphin    parrot |

3. A _____ is a colorful bird.

4. A _____ is a mammal that lives in the sea.

**E** Read the clues. Write the word.

1. This animal has one or two round parts on its back.

   _____

2. This animal hops from place to place.

   _____

# Write

**Remember!**
Use headings to organize information.

**Circle the headings.**

**Parrots**

Parrots are colorful birds that live mostly in warm countries.

**What they eat**

Parrots eat insects and plants. Seeds are their favorite food.

# Read

**READING GOAL:**
**Identify the Theme**

**Remember!**
To find the **theme**, ask, *What did the character learn? What did I learn?*

---

**A** Read the story. Think about what the character learned while you read.

## Helping Eva

Eva and Miles wanted to go to the aquarium, but first they had to help their parents with some chores.

"Eva, you cut the grass. Miles, you wash the car," said Dad. "When you're done, we'll go."

Miles began washing the car. Eva sat on the grass. She didn't want to work. She wanted to go to the aquarium.

When Miles finished washing the car, Eva was looking at the clouds. "It looks like a dolphin," Eva said, pointing.

"Let me help you," said Miles. But Eva didn't respond.

Miles started to cut the grass. Eva studied the clouds. Finally, Eva got up and helped Miles. Soon they finished the chores.

"Mom! Dad!" they called together. "Now we're ready to go to the aquarium!"

**B** Choose the correct answer.

1. Miles was kind and helped Eva with her chores.
   - ☐ a. true    ☐ b. false    ☐ c. doesn't say

2. Eva and Miles wanted to go to the zoo.
   - ☐ a. true    ☐ b. false    ☐ c. doesn't say

3. Miles had to wash the car.
   - ☐ a. true    ☐ b. false    ☐ c. doesn't say

4. Eva wanted to walk the dog.
   - ☐ a. true    ☐ b. false    ☐ c. doesn't say

5. Eva saw a cloud that looked like a dolphin.
   - ☐ a. true    ☐ b. false    ☐ c. doesn't say

6. Miles had to do both chores by himself because Eva didn't want to work.
   - ☐ a. true    ☐ b. false    ☐ c. doesn't say

**C** Answer the questions. Use full sentences.

1. What did Eva and Miles have to do before they could go to the aquarium?

   _____

2. What did Eva do while her brother cut the grass?

   _____

3. Why did Miles help Eva?

   _____

4. Do you think the family went to the aquarium? Why or why not?

   _____

**D** Read the text. Choose the correct word to fill each blank.

### All Aboard

Sailors aboard large ships have lots of chores to do each day.
Every morning, they (1) _____ and get up early. They all share chores. In the
morning some sailors (2) _____ for breakfast with clean forks and knives,
while the others (3) _____ healthy food. After they eat, some sailors clear
the table and (4) _____. Everyone has to work together to get the ship ready
for sailing!

1. ☐ a. walk the dog
   ☐ b. set the alarm
   ☐ c. cut the grass

2. ☐ a. set the table
   ☐ b. buy groceries
   ☐ c. put away the groceries

3. ☐ a. wash the dishes
   ☐ b. walk the dog
   ☐ c. cook

4. ☐ a. cook
   ☐ b. wash the dishes
   ☐ c. set the alarm

**E** Unscramble and match.

1. a w l k  h e t  g o d •

   _____

2. a s h w  e t h  a c r •

   _____

• a. when you take your pet
     outside to get exercise

• b. you do this outside with
     a bucket, water, and soap

# Read

**READING GOAL:**
**Identify Cause and Effect**

**A** Read the advertisement. Identify cause and effect while you read.

## Rosie Does It All

Take our special robot, Rosie, home for one week and watch how she cleans your whole house in almost no time! Don't miss this special offer. Continue reading to see what Rosie can do for you.

Imagine you leave your windows open during a rainstorm. The floor gets wet and the windows get dirty. Now you have to wash the windows and mop the floor. No problem! Rosie can do it. She can even dust the furniture at the same time. Rosie can do everything but your homework!

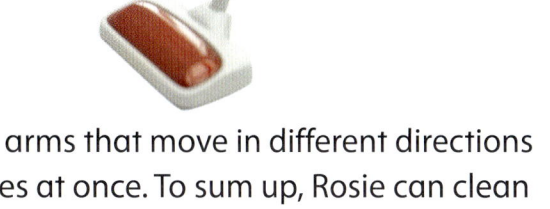

She can do all of this because Rosie has four arms that move in different directions at the same time. She can do up to four chores at once. To sum up, Rosie can clean up your whole house quickly, so you have time to do your homework!

**B** Choose the correct answer.

1. What is the advertisement for?
   - [ ] a. a robot
   - [ ] b. a mop
   - [ ] c. a bucket

2. What happens when you leave your windows open during a rainstorm?
   - [ ] a. The floor gets wet.
   - [ ] b. The windows get dirty.
   - [ ] c. both of the above

3. How many jobs can Rosie do at the same time?
   - [ ] a. two
   - [ ] b. four
   - [ ] c. six

4. Why can Rosie do so many jobs at once?
   - [ ] a. She has two arms.
   - [ ] b. She has four arms.
   - [ ] c. She has six arms.

**C** Complete the sentences with one, two, or three words.

1. This text is an _____ for a robot.

2. It suggests you try out the robot at home for one _____

3. It says Rosie can clean your whole house _____

4. Rosie can _____ and mop the floor at the same time.

5. Rosie can do everything but _____

6. Rosie has four arms that move in _____ at the same time.

**D** Choose the words that complete the sentence.

| dust the furniture    wash the windows |

1. After a rainstorm, Rosie can _____

2. Rosie probably uses a cloth to _____

| buy groceries    put away the groceries |

3. You can _____ at the supermarket.

4. When you get home from the supermarket, you _____

**E** Read the clues. Write the phrase.

1. When you put things in the correct place on a table where you work.

_____

2. This is when you fix sheets and blankets from sleeping last night.

_____

3. This is when you use soap and water to clean where you walk.

_____

# Write

**Remember!**
To begin your conclusion, use phrases such as *in conclusion* and *to sum up*.

**Which sentences have a phrase that begins the conclusion?**
**Circle the phrases.**

1. In conclusion, there is nothing better than a robot to do your chores for you.

2. To sum up, Rosie can do your chores while you do your homework.

3. Wouldn't it be great to have a robot that could do your chores for you?

# Read

**READING GOAL:**
**Skim for Gist**

**Remember!**
Before you read, quickly look at the story's title, the first and last sentence of each paragraph, and pictures to learn what the story is about.

**A**  Skim the text. Think about the gist of the story. Then read the invitation.

# Our Class Picnic

Our class is going to have a picnic for the beginning of spring. It will be at Elm Street Park on Saturday. If the weather is good, everyone will meet in the picnic area next to the river. There will be lots of delicious foods to eat. We will probably have a barbecue and grill burgers.

After lunch, there will be lots of fun activities. Some students want to go hiking. Others like playing volleyball. There is a sign-up sheet in the classroom.

Don't forget to sign up for your favorite outdoor activity!

| NAME | ACTIVITY |
|------|----------|
| Zoe | go hiking |
| ALEX | CANOE ON THE RIVER |
| Hugo | fly a kite |
| Alicia | do a treasure hunt |
| Matt | play volleyball |

**B**  Choose the correct answer.

1. The gist of the story is that the class is having a picnic.
   ☐ a. true  ☐ b. false  ☐ c. doesn't say

2. They are having a picnic for the end of the school year.
   ☐ a. true  ☐ b. false  ☐ c. doesn't say

3. The students will meet at the beach.
   ☐ a. true  ☐ b. false  ☐ c. doesn't say

4. There will be bottles of soda to drink.
   ☐ a. true  ☐ b. false  ☐ c. doesn't say

5. After lunch, the students will do outdoor activities.
   ☐ a. true  ☐ b. false  ☐ c. doesn't say

6. Students can write their names and favorite activities on a sign-up sheet in the classroom.
   ☐ a. true  ☐ b. false  ☐ c. doesn't say

**C** Answer the questions. Use full sentences.

1. Why is the class having a picnic?

   _____

2. When and where will they meet?

   _____

3. What will they probably eat?

   _____

4. What should they sign-up for?

   _____

**D** Read the text. Choose the correct word to fill each blank.

### I Love Summer

My favorite season is (1) _____ because it is hot and I can (2) _____. I like swimming in the ocean and collecting shells on the beach.

(3) _____ is my mom's favorite season because the flowers bloom. She likes taking a tent and sleeping bags and (4) _____ under the stars. My dad and I like taking our paddles and canoeing on the river.

1. ☐ a. spring
   ☐ b. summer
   ☐ c. winter

2. ☐ a. go ice skating
   ☐ b. build a snowman
   ☐ c. go to the beach

3. ☐ a. Spring
   ☐ b. Summer
   ☐ c. Winter

4. ☐ a. climbing a mountain
   ☐ b. going camping
   ☐ c. canoeing on the river

**E** Unscramble and match.

1. o g  i h i k n g •
   _____

2. o c a n e  n o  a  i r e r v •
   _____

3. a v h e  a  p i c c i n •
   _____

• a. go on a long walk in the country

• b. move through water in a small boat

• c. eat a meal outside

# Read

**READING GOAL:**
**Draw Conclusions**

**Remember!**
While you read, use words and pictures in a text and your own knowledge to **draw conclusions** about what the writer doesn't tell you.

**A** Read. Draw conclusions while you read.

Dear Alexis,

Winter is my favorite season. Here in northern Norway it's very cold and snowy in winter. We are expecting a winter storm this afternoon. If the winds get stronger, it could be a blizzard. It's good weather for staying at home and drinking hot chocolate.

The best thing about winter is not skiing or skating on the lakes when they freeze. It is seeing the Northern Lights. These are colored lights that move across the sky over the North Pole. They are usually green and pink, but they can be red, blue, yellow, and violet, too. The best time to see them is between October and March, so I wish you could come then!

Your friend,

Leif

**B** Choose the correct answer.

1. Next winter, what will Leif want to do first?

   ☐ a. go see the Northern Lights

   ☐ b. go to the beach

   ☐ c. go hiking

2. What is a blizzard?

   ☐ a. a windstorm

   ☐ b. a snowstorm with strong winds

   ☐ c. a rainstorm

3. What does Leif like to do during a blizzard?

   ☐ a. go skiing

   ☐ b. go ice skating

   ☐ c. stay home and drink hot chocolate

4. What colors are the Northern Lights?

   ☐ a. black and white

   ☐ b. brown and orange

   ☐ c. green and pink

**C** Complete the sentences with one, two, or three words.

1. Leif writes a _____ to his friend Alexis.

2. In northern Norway, it is very cold and snowy in _____

3. In winter, the lakes _____ and people go ice skating.

4. During a _____, Leif likes to stay home and drink hot chocolate.

5. The Northern Lights are _____ that move across the sky over the North Pole.

6. You can see the Northern Lights in Norway between _____

**D** Choose a word and complete the sentence.

| fall   winter |

1. In _____ it is cold and snowy.

2. In _____ the leaves change color.

| blizzard   freeze |

3. When it is very cold, the water in a lake will _____

4. A snowstorm with strong winds is a _____

**E** Read the clues. Write the word or phrase.

1. This is when you move over snow on long, flat things.

   _____

2. You can have fun doing this on a frozen lake with special boots.

   _____

3. You do this when you travel around a new place to learn about it.

   _____

# Write

**Circle the words that connect two complete sentences.**

1. I like to ski, and my brother likes to ice skate.

2. Skating is fun, but the Northern Lights are amazing!

3. I don't have skis, so I can't go skiing.

**Remember!**
Use a comma and words like *and*, *but*, and *so* to connect two complete sentences.

# Read

**READING GOAL:**
**Scan for Details**

**A** Read. Scan the text for numbers after you read.

## Making Kimchi

Kimchi is a Korean dish made with cabbage. There are many ways to make kimchi. Mom and I like to make fresh and crunchy kimchi.

Here is our recipe:

### Fresh Kimchi

1 cabbage
a little garlic
some dry Korean red pepper
2 spoons of fish sauce
1 spoon of sesame oil
sugar
salt

In a bowl, mix salt and sugar in one liter of warm water. Stir with a spoon. Add cabbage and wait 30 minutes.

Pour out the water. Put the cabbage in a large bowl with garlic, red pepper, fish sauce, and sesame oil. Mix. Wait 30 minutes and eat!

**B** Choose the correct answer.

1. I can scan the recipe to see how many spoons of fish sauce I should use to make kimchi.

   ☐ a. true      ☐ b. false      ☐ c. doesn't say

2. Kimchi is a Korean dish made with cucumbers.

   ☐ a. true      ☐ b. false      ☐ c. doesn't say

3. Fresh kimchi is crunchy.

   ☐ a. true      ☐ b. false      ☐ c. doesn't say

4. Fresh kimchi tastes sour after a week.

   ☐ a. true      ☐ b. false      ☐ c. doesn't say

5. After mixing together all the ingredients, they wait 45 minutes.

   ☐ a. true      ☐ b. false      ☐ c. doesn't say

**C** Answer the questions. Use full sentences.

1.  How would you describe kimchi?

    _____

2.  How much fish sauce do you need to make kimchi?

    _____

3.  How much cabbage do they use when they make kimchi?

    _____

4.  What do they mix with the cabbage?

    _____

**D** Read the text. Choose the correct word to fill each blank.

### Hanjan Restaurant

Hanjan Restaurant serves the best Korean food in town. Their curry is
(1) _____, and their sweet and sour chicken (2) _____ delicious. They have
several noodle dishes.
Rice noodles are (3) _____, but fried noodles are sometimes (4) _____.
Dinner is served from 5:00 p.m. to 8:00 p.m. Be sure to come with the
whole family!

1.  ☐ a. soft
    ☐ b. spicy
    ☐ c. sour

2.  ☐ a. plays
    ☐ b. cooks
    ☐ c. tastes

3.  ☐ a. soft
    ☐ b. sweet
    ☐ c. crunchy

4.  ☐ a. warm
    ☐ b. crunchy
    ☐ c. soft

**E** Unscramble and match.

1.  m l l e s •

    _____

2.  w e e t s •

    _____

3.  o u s r •

    _____

• a. candy, pie, cupcakes, and
      chocolate are all this

• b. use your nose to do this

• c. how a lemon tastes

# Read

**READING GOAL:**
**Visualize**

**Remember!**
Notice the words the writer uses to describe things. Try to see those things in your mind.

**A** Read. Visualize while you read.

# Dogs Have Amazing Hearing

Look at your dog. Its body is still. It moves his head to one side and raises its ears. It hears something.

Dogs have excellent hearing. They can hear sounds like whistles that humans cannot hear. They can also hear sounds almost four times farther away than humans can. Has your dog ever barked when you did not hear anything? Then a minute later someone rang your doorbell? Your dog heard the person coming first!

Dogs have more than eighteen muscles in their ears, so they can move them in many directions. They can actually hear different sounds at the same time!

The next time your dog moves its head to one side and raises its ears, listen carefully. It is telling you it has heard something.

**B** Choose the correct answer.

1. How does a dog look like when it hears a sound?
   - [ ] a. its head is to one side and its ears are up
   - [ ] b. its ears are down
   - [ ] c. it stands on two legs

2. What sounds can dogs hear that humans cannot hear?
   - [ ] a. bells
   - [ ] b. whistles
   - [ ] c. horns

3. How many muscles do dogs have in their ears?
   - [ ] a more than twelve
   - [ ] b. more than eighteen
   - [ ] c. more than 24

4. What is a dog telling you when it moves its head to one side and raises its ears?
   - [ ] a. It smells something.
   - [ ] b. It tastes something.
   - [ ] c. It hears something.

**C** Complete the sentences with one, two, or three words.

1. When a dog hears a sound, it _____ to one side.

2. Dogs have excellent _____

3. Dogs can hear sounds almost _____ farther away than humans.

4. Dogs can move their ears _____ to hear different sounds at the same time.

5. Sometimes dogs bark to tell you they _____ something.

6. _____ when a dog shows he has heard something.

**D** Choose a word and complete the sentence.

> look   listen

1. A dog can _____ with its sensitive ears.

2. A dog opens its eyes wide to _____ at another animal.

> hear   touch

3. A dog can _____ sounds that humans cannot hear.

4. You should never _____ another person's dog.

**E** Read the clues. Write the word or phrase.

1. When you hear something that reminds you of another sound.

   _____

2. This is a word to describe something that is very good.

   _____

3. When you touch something and it reminds you of something else you touched.

   _____

# Write

**Remember!**
Use your five senses to describe your topic.

Circle the sentence that paints a picture in your mind.

1. I always enjoy a day at the beach.

2. I like to make kimchi.

3. The cat was brown and white with a black patch around its left eye.

# Read

**READING GOAL:**
**Take Notes**

**A** Read. Take notes while you read.

Street foods are very popular in China. Street vendors in different parts of China sell different kinds of foods.

In the streets of Shanghai, people eat noodles, pancakes, and grilled meat. They also enjoy sweet dishes, like sweet egg cakes.

In the streets in Sichuan province, street vendors sell a lot of spicy foods. Tofu with hot chili sauce is a popular dish. Hotpot, a meat soup, is popular, too. People hold pieces of meat and vegetables with their chopsticks and cook them in the hot soup.

China is growing and changing, and so are the street vendors. Who knows how long you will be able to taste street food in China? Hurry and try the delicious foods before they disappear!

Chinese **Street Food**

**B** Choose the correct answer.

1. The fact that street vendors in Sichuan province sell spicy food is an important detail.
   ☐ a. true  ☐ b. false  ☐ c. doesn't say

2. All street vendors in China sell the same foods.
   ☐ a. true  ☐ b. false  ☐ c. doesn't say

3. In Shanghai people eat pancakes and grilled meat.
   ☐ a. true  ☐ b. false  ☐ c. doesn't say

4. Hotpot is a meat soup with meat and vegetables.
   ☐ a. true  ☐ b. false  ☐ c. doesn't say

5. Sweet egg cakes are popular in Sichuan province.
   ☐ a. true  ☐ b. false  ☐ c. doesn't say

6. The restaurants serve the same food as the street vendors.
   ☐ a. true  ☐ b. false  ☐ c. doesn't say

**C** Answer the questions. Use full sentences.

1. What street foods are popular in Sichuan province?

_____

2. How do people cook pieces of meat and vegetables in a hotpot?

_____

3. What is street food like in Shanghai?

_____

4. What street foods would you like to try? Why?

_____

**D** Read the text. Choose the correct word to fill each blank.

### The Royal Palm Hotel, Cairo

Are you planning a trip to (1) _____? Come and stay at the Royal Palm Hotel in Cairo. The hotel has two pools and lots of activities. Every day there is a trip to (2) _____. If you want, the hotel can also arrange for you to (3) _____. The hotel has three restaurants, but it is fun to visit Cairo and buy food from a (4) _____. They serve delicious kebabs!

1. ☐ a. China
   ☐ b. Egypt
   ☐ c. Hawaii

2. ☐ a. see the pyramids
   ☐ b. play softball
   ☐ c. fly a kite

3. ☐ a. surf the waves
   ☐ b. go skiing
   ☐ c. ride a camel

4. ☐ a. street vendor
   ☐ b. driver
   ☐ c. pilot

**E** Unscramble and match.

1. H w a a i i •                          • a. a place in the United States that
_____                              has beautiful beaches

2. h o p c i k c t s s •                  • b. thin sticks used to eat, but not
_____                              a fork

3. C i h a n •                           • c. a soft, white food
_____

4. o u f t •                             • d. a very large country in Asia
_____

# Read

**READING GOAL:**
**Identify characters, setting, and plot**

**A** Read. Identify characters, setting, and plot while you read.

# The Grasshopper and the Ant

One summer day, in a town in Mexico, a grasshopper was sitting in the sun playing the guitar. A tiny ant walked by carrying a big plate of tacos. The ant was hot and tired because she had been working for days.

"Come sing with me," said the grasshopper.

"I can't," said the ant. "I have to cook tacos now and save them for the winter when it will be too cold to cook outside."

Finally, winter came. The ant had plenty of food, but the grasshopper was hungry. He had nothing to eat. Luckily, the ant was kind and gave him something.

Together they ate the tacos the ant had prepared over those hot summer days. The grasshopper learned that it is important to plan ahead.

**B** Choose the correct answer.

1. Who are the characters in this story?
   - [ ] a. an ant and a lizard
   - [ ] b. a lizard and a grasshopper
   - [ ] c. an ant and a grasshopper

2. What does the ant do in the summer?
   - [ ] a. She cooks crepes to eat in the winter.
   - [ ] b. She cooks tacos to eat in the winter.
   - [ ] c. She sings and plays the guitar.

3. What does the grasshopper do while the ant cooks tacos?
   - [ ] a. He plays the guitar.
   - [ ] b. He plays the trombone.
   - [ ] c. He cuts the grass.

4. How does the ant help the grasshopper in the winter?
   - [ ] a. She gives him food to eat.
   - [ ] b. She gives him a sweater to wear.
   - [ ] c. She plays the guitar so he can sing.

**C** Complete the sentences with one, two, or three words.

1.  The setting is summer and winter in a town in _____

2.  The grasshopper _____ and sings.

3.  The tiny ant cooks _____

4.  The ant is cooking food in the summer to eat _____

5.  In the winter, _____ has no food.

6.  The ant is _____ and she gives the grasshopper something to eat.

**D** Choose a word and complete the sentence.

> Tacos    Crepes

1.  _____ are thin pancakes that are popular in France.

2.  _____ are thin pancakes made from corn with meat and vegetables inside.

> beautiful    rickshaw

3.  A _____ is a form of transportation in India.

4.  There are many _____ places to visit around the world.

**E** Read the clues. Write the word.

1.  In this country, you can eat tacos from street vendors.

    _____

2.  In this country, you can eat crepes from street vendors.

    _____

3.  In this country, you can ride rickshaws.

    _____

# Write

**Remember!**
Use pronouns to avoid repeating names.

Circle the pronouns.

1.  Nabil and Emily rode in a rickshaw. They were scared.

2.  Rob went to Egypt. He rode a camel.

3.  Alison likes Mexican food. She ate two tacos for lunch.

# Dictionary

Definitions based on the *Oxford Basic American Dictionary for Learners of English.*

## B

**bag** *noun* a thing made of cloth, paper, leather, etc., for holding and carrying things: *a bag of potato chips/bags of pretzels*

**beach** *noun* a piece of land next to an ocean or a lake that is covered with sand or stones: *go to the beach*

**bean** *noun* a seed, or a seed container, that we use as food

**beautiful** *adj.* very nice to see, hear, or smell

**blizzard** *noun* a very bad storm with snow and strong winds

**bottle** *noun* a glass or plastic container for liquids, with a thin part at the top: *a bottle of water/bottles of soda*

**box** *noun* a container with straight sides. A box often has a lid: *a box of chocolates*

**butterfly** *noun* an insect with big wings that usually have bright colors

## C

**camel** *noun* a large animal with one or two round parts (called humps) on its back. Camels carry people and things in hot dry places: *ride a camel*

**camp** *verb* to live in a kind of small house made of cloth (called a tent) for a short time: *go camping*

**canoe** *verb* to move through the water in a light, narrow boat using a flat piece of wood (called a paddle): *canoe on the river*

**caterpillar** *noun* a small animal with a long thin body and many legs that changes into an insect that flies (called a butterfly)

**cheetah** *noun* a large wild cat that comes from Africa and can run very fast

**China** *noun* a very large country in eastern Asia

**chopsticks** *noun* a pair of thin sticks that are used for eating with, especially in some Asian countries

**clean** *verb* to put everything in its correct place and take away things that should not be in a place: *clean the desk*

**clean up** *phrasal verb* to remove all the dirt or pick up all the things from a place: *clean up my room*

**climb** *verb* to go up toward the top of something: *climb a mountain*

**cook** *verb* to make food ready to eat by heating it

**crepe** *noun* a thin round type of food that is like a pancake

**crunchy** *adj.* hard and dry, so that it makes a noise when you eat it or walk on it

**cup** *noun* a small round container with a handle, which you can drink from: *a cup of coffee*

**cupcake** *noun* a small, round cake for one person

**curry** *noun* an Indian dish of meat or vegetables cooked with spices and often eaten with rice

## D

**dish** *noun* a container for food. You can use a dish to cook food in an oven, or to put food on the table: *wash the dishes*

**dolphin** *noun* an intelligent animal that lives in the ocean

**dust** *verb* to take dust off something with a cloth: *dust the furniture*

## E

**Egypt** *noun* a country in northern Africa

**explore** *verb* to travel around a new place to learn about it

## F

**fall** *noun* the part of the year between summer and winter

**faster** *adj.* moving, happening, or doing something more quickly than something else

**feel** *verb* used for saying how something seems when you touch it: *The trombone feels like a trumpet, but it is bigger*

**France** *noun* a country in western Europe

**freeze** *verb* to be very cold

# Dictionary

## G

**gazelle** *noun* an African animal that looks like a small deer and can run very fast

**glass** *noun* a thing made of glass that you drink from: *a glass of milk*

**grass** *noun* a plant with thin green leaves that covers fields and yards: *cut the grass*

**groceries** *noun* food and other things for the home that you buy regularly: *buy groceries*

## H

**Hawaii** *noun* a U.S. state in the Pacific Ocean

**hear** *verb* to notice sounds with your ears

**help** *verb* to do something useful for someone: *help my parents*

**hike** *verb* to go on a long walk in the country: *go hiking*

**hot chocolate** *noun* a drink made by mixing chocolate powder with hot water or milk: *drink hot chocolate*

## I

**ice skate** *verb* to move on ice in special boots (called ice skates) which have long sharp pieces of metal on the bottom

**India** *noun* a large country in southern Asia

## J

**jaguar** *noun* a large wild cat with black spots that lives in Central and South America

## K

**kangaroo** *noun* an Australian mammal that jumps on its strong back legs and carries its babies in a pocket on its front

## L

**larger** *adj.* bigger than something you are comparing it to

**like** *prep.* the same as someone or something

**listen** *verb* to hear something when you are trying to hear it

**lizard** *noun* a small animal that has four legs, a long tail, and rough skin

**look** *verb* to appear

## M

**make the bed** *verb* to arrange the sheets and blankets so that they are smooth and the bed is ready for someone to sleep in: *make the bed*

**meatballs** *noun* small round balls of meat

**Mexico** *noun* a country in southern North America

**mop** *verb* to wash floors using a thing with a long handle (called a mop): *mop the floor*

## N

**noodles** *noun* long thin pieces of food made from flour, egg, and water that are cooked in water or used in soups

**nut** *noun* a dry fruit that has a hard outside part with a seed inside: *a bowl of nuts*

## P

**parrot** *noun* a bird with very bright feathers that can copy what people say

**picnic** *noun* a meal that you eat outside, away from home: *have a picnic*

**piece** *noun* a part of something: *a piece of pizza/a piece of cheese*

**polar bear** *noun* a large white animal that lives near the North Pole

**pretty** *adj.* attractive and pleasant to listen to

**put away** *phrasal verb* to put something back in its usual place: *put away the groceries*

**pyramid** *noun* a building with a flat bottom and three or four sides that come to a point at the top: *see the pyramids*

## R

**rickshaw** *noun* a small, light vehicle with two wheels used in some Asian countries to carry passengers. A rickshaw is pulled by someone walking or riding a bicycle

## S

**set** *verb* [1] to make something ready to use, or to make something start working: *set the alarm* [2] to put knives, forks, plates, and other things on the table before you eat: *set the table*

**ski** *verb* to move over snow on a pair of long flat pieces of wood, metal, or plastic (called skis) that you attach to boots: *go skiing*

**smaller** *adj.* not as big as something you are comparing it to

**smell** *verb* to have a particular smell: *The cookies smell like butter.*

**soft** *adj.* not hard or firm; that moves when you press it

**sound** *verb* to seem a particular way when you hear it

**sour** *adj.* with a sharp taste like a lemon

**spicy** *adj.* having a strong taste because spices have been used to add flavor to it

**spring** *noun* the part of the year after winter, when plants start to grow

**squirrel** *noun* a small gray, brown, or black animal with a big, thick tail

**street vendor** *noun* a person who sells things on the street

**summer** *noun* the part of the year between spring and fall

**sushi** *noun* a Japanese dish of small portions of cold cooked rice, served with raw fish or vegetables on top

**sweet** *adj.* containing or tasting of sugar

**taco** *noun* a Mexican food that is a thin, crisp pancake filled with meat, cheese, and tomatoes

**taste** *verb* to feel or know a particular food or drink in your mouth

**tofu** *noun* a soft, white substance that is made from a type of bean and used in cooking, often instead of meat

**touch** *verb* to put a part of your body, usually your hand or finger, onto someone or something

**visit** *verb* to go to see a person or place for a short time: *visit family*

**walk** *verb* to make an animal walk somewhere: *walk the dog*

**wash** *verb* to clean someone, something, or yourself with water: *wash the dishes/wash the car/wash the windows*

**window** *noun* an opening in a building or in a car door, for example, with glass in it

**winter** *noun* the coldest part of the year, which comes between fall and spring

**wonderful** *adj.* very good

# Syllabus

| Topic | Unit | Reading Goal | Key Words | Writing Goal |
|---|---|---|---|---|
| **TOPIC 1** Let's Eat! | Unit 1 | Paraphrase | *bean, a bag of potato chips, a piece of pizza, a glass of milk, a cup of coffee, a bottle of water, a piece of cheese, a box of chocolates* | Write an explanatory text |
| | Unit 2 | Use the 5 Ws | *cupcake, bags of pretzels, nut, sushi, noodles, meatballs, curry, bottles of soda* | Focus: Transitions |
| **TOPIC 2** The Animal Kingdom | Unit 3 | Make connections | *smaller, squirrel, lizard, larger, jaguar, polar bear, caterpillar, butterfly* | Write a report |
| | Unit 4 | Classify and categorize | *kangaroo, gazelle, parrot, cheetah, camel, faster, fastest, dolphin* | Focus: Headings |
| **TOPIC 3** Around the House | Unit 5 | Identify the theme | *help my parents, set the alarm, walk the dog, set the table, cook, wash the dishes, cut the grass, wash the car* | Write an essay |
| | Unit 6 | Identify cause and effect | *clean up my room, mop the floor, clean the desk, dust the furniture, make the bed, wash the windows, buy groceries, put away the groceries* | Focus: Concluding phrases |
| **TOPIC 4** The Four Seasons | Unit 7 | Skim for gist | *summer, go to the beach, go camping, go hiking, climb a mountain, have a picnic, spring, canoe on the river* | Write an opinion essay |
| | Unit 8 | Draw conclusions | *explore, fall, winter, blizzard, ice skate, go skiing, drink hot chocolate, freeze* | Focus: Connectors |
| **TOPIC 5** Our Five Senses | Unit 9 | Scan for details | *smell, smell like, taste, soft, sweet, crunchy, sour, spicy* | Write a descriptive essay |
| | Unit 10 | Visualize | *look, touch, sound like, hear, wonderful, listen, feel like, pretty* | Focus: Senses to describe |
| **TOPIC 6** See the World! | Unit 11 | Take notes | *Hawaii, China, tofu, chopsticks, Egypt, street vendor, see the pyramids, ride a camel* | Write a story |
| | Unit 12 | Identify characters, setting, and plot | *Mexico, visit family, beautiful, taco, crepe, France, India, rickshaw* | Focus: Pronouns |